Good
Business

Putting Spiritual Principles
Into Practice at Work

Edited by
Charlotte Shelton and Martha Lynn

Good Business

Putting Spiritual Principles Into Practice at Work

Edited by

Charlotte Shelton and Martha Lynn

Unity Village, MO 64065-0001

Good Business

First Edition 2010

Copyright © 2010 by Unity School of Christianity. All rights reserved. No part of this book may be used or reproduced in any manner whatsoever without written permission from Unity House except in the case of brief quotations embedded in critical articles and reviews or in the newsletters and lesson plans of licensed Unity teachers and ministers. Permission must be obtained from individual copyright owners identified herein. For information, address Unity House, 1901 NW Blue Parkway, Unity Village, MO 64065-0001.

Unity House books are available at special discounts for bulk purchases for study groups, book clubs, sales promotions, book signings or fundraising. To place an order, call the Unity Customer Care Department at 800-251-3571 or e-mail *sales@unityonline.org*.

Bible quotations are from the New Revised Standard Version unless otherwise noted.

Cover design by: Karen Rizzo

Interior design by: The Covington Group

Library of Congress Control Number: 2010920261

ISBN 978-0-87159-344-3

Canada BN 13252 0933 RT

Contents

Acknowledgements ix

Dedication: Ebby Halliday xi

Introduction 1

DEFINING GOOD BUSINESS

1. Service and Satisfaction 9
   Brian Tracy

2. Corporate Social Responsibility: The Foundation
   of Good Business 16
   Corinne McLaughlin

3. Spiritual Wholeness: Operationalizing the Intangible. . . 28
   Daryl Conner

4. Companies That Care 52
   Riane Eisler

SOULFUL LEADERS

5. Soul Management 61
   Bil and Cher Holton

6. The Power of the Seven Cs. 69
   John Knowles

7. The Path of Leadership Progress 79
   Stephen Blumberg

8. Executive Evocateurs 85
   John Schuster

ᕲ

9. Reconstructing Our Idea of Leadership 90
   Peter Block

10. The New Leadership Agenda 97
    Richard Barrett

11. The Leader as Spiritual Agent 107
    Margaret Wheatley

DESIGNING SPIRITED ORGANIZATIONS

12. Becoming an Employer of Choice.................. 115
    Leigh Branham

13. Spirit at Work 122
    Val Kinjerski

14. The Power of a Values-Based Culture 132
    Susan Mundy Beck

15. Good Business in Tough Economic Times........... 143
    Margaret Benefiel and Debora Jackson

CONSCIOUS CONTRIBUTORS

16. The Power of Choice............................ 155
    Jim Bearden

17. Great Expectations = Great Success 165
    Judy Zerafa

18. Keep Your Eye on the Doughnut 170
    Ruth Ann Harnisch

19. The Six Characteristics of Successful People......... 177
    Tom Hill

20. CRAVE Your Goals!............................ 182
    Tricia Molloy

Contents

❧

NEW SKILLS FOR A NEW MILLENNIUM

21. Say "Yes" to What Really Matters.................. 191
    Martha Lynn

22. Quantum Skills for a New Millennium 199
    Charlotte Shelton

SUMMARY

Doing Well and Doing Good 223
    Charlotte Shelton and Martha Lynn

RESOURCES

What Is Unity? 231

Good Business Magazine: Articles From the
Great Depression 233

   • The Chance of a Lifetime...................... 234

   • Blessings in Disguise 238

   • Any Job You Want............................. 242

Daily Affirmations for Good Business 248

Good Business Clubs............................... 252

Endnotes 257

About the Editors 263

☙

Good Business

Acknowledgements

We are deeply grateful to the all the authors who brought their wisdom and expertise to *Good Business*. Without their generosity and loving spirit, our book would have remained just a dream. Thanks to our contributors, we now have an anthology of practical spiritual tools that readers can begin using immediately to create more meaningful workplaces and more successful careers. The deep respect and appreciation we feel for our contributing authors will only expand as you, our readers, are blessed by their gifts.

Our gratitude extends to two women who enrich our lives every day: Sandy Meyer, executive assistant to Unity's president and CEO (Charlotte), and Sandy Drake, executive assistant to the vice president of SpiritPath (Martha). Besides being exemplary customer-service role models, their assistance throughout the writing of this book has been beyond measure. They also are the glue that keeps our weekly Unity.FM radio program, *Good Business*, running smoothly.

We are deeply grateful to the Unity House editorial and production team: Paula Coppel, vice president of communications; Stephanie Stokes Oliver, editorial director; and Sharon Sartin, production assistant. This team's feedback enhanced the book's readability while keeping its message and structure intact.

We also extend a big thank-you to the staff that edited and designed the book. We appreciate the creative contributions of Terry Newell and Unity's New Media department to the book's look and feel. There would be no book at all without our Unity.FM producer, Denise Blake. She is solely responsible for booking the wonderful guests whose spiritual business savvy will be shared in the following pages. Denise, thank you for a job well done!

I (Martha) would also like to thank my beloved husband, Ron Lynn, who always keeps faith in me no matter what projects I take on. He is my loving mirror and reminds me who I am even when difficult times present. And thank you to my son, Aaron Lynn, and daughter-in-law, Dr. Rachael Rzasa Lynn, whose compassion and clarity of purpose provide me with constant hope that good business can be a universal reality in my lifetime.

I (Charlotte) want to thank my dad, Okley Kinder, who taught me much about leadership as I observed his business management and community service contributions—and who made his life transition while we were working on this book project. I also want to thank my husband, Dr. Jim Moore, for giving me the "space" to write, and my children, Dr. Matthew Shelton and Laura Shelton Garfield, for loving and supporting me through all my many projects. Finally, I thank my four beautiful grandchildren for energizing my life and igniting in me the desire to help create healthier workplaces for future generations.

We thank you, our readers, for your commitment to model universal spiritual principles in your organizations. Together we are creating ethical, accountable, responsible, collaborative, service-oriented, vision-focused and mission-based businesses. We are the ones we have been waiting for. We are changing the world of work—one decision at a time.

Abundant blessings,

Martha Lynn and Charlotte Shelton

Unity Village, Missouri

Dedication

This book is dedicated to Ebby Halliday, the first lady of Texas real estate and a long-time friend of Unity. At age 98, Ebby still goes to work every day in the offices of her Dallas, Texas, real estate company—a company she founded in 1945 and grew to more than $48 billion in annual sales with 29 offices and 1,600 sales agents.

Michael Poss, the author of a 2009 biography about Ebby, writes in the foreword to the book: "Football and real estate have a lot in common. Leadership matters. Ambition counts. Heart energizes. Ebby Halliday might have made a good quarterback. Her intriguing story reflects her ambition to achieve despite all obstacles, her great heart that led her to reach out to associates and customers, and her leadership that made her a role model." In the book's preface Ebby lists her recipe for a meaningful life:

1. Maintain your health.

2. Keep learning.

3. Choose a career wisely.

4. Learn to communicate.

5. Build your self-confidence.

6. Create good business habits.

7. Observe company policies.

8. Express gratitude by thanking people.

9. Contribute to your community.

10. Choose your partner carefully.

We believe that Ebby's recommendations are not only the recipe for a meaningful life, they are also the recipe for good business.

Thank you, Ebby, for leading the way—for women in business and for all business leaders who want to bring universal spiritual principles into the workplace.

Introduction

"There is nothing better for a man than to rejoice in his work."
—Ecclesiastes 3:22

Many people may think that the phrase "good business" is an oxymoron. Such people have typically either had a painful experience in the workplace or they have let their view of business be shaped by the media. We don't question that many employees have been treated poorly at work by bully bosses or dysfunctional co-workers. We don't deny that materialistic managers and ego-driven CEOs have committed crimes against their employees, shareholders and society. However, we do believe these horror stories are the exception, not the norm. While the media focuses on stories like Enron, WorldCom, Lehman Brothers, Bernard L. Madoff Investment Securities and AIG, many other organizations are functioning at much higher levels of consciousness. They are doing good business.

We love the phrase "good business," and so did Unity's founders, Charles and Myrtle Fillmore—they even published a magazine by that name. In the first issue of *Good Business*, the editor Frank Martinek wrote: "Never in the history of the world has it been so necessary for good business, from the smallest unit to the largest, to prevail. As we know, God is good, and since all business is God's business, good business is most essential for real progress and prosperity."[1] Note that this was written in 1933—in the throes of the Great Depression; yet we believe this comment is equally applicable to the economic challenges that businesses are facing almost 80 years later.

Good business is essential for progress and prosperity. And we at Unity world headquarters want to do our part in modeling, encouraging and supporting good business. Though Unity no longer publishes *Good Business* magazine, we (Martha and Charlotte) host a weekly Internet radio program on Unity.FM by this same name. On this radio program we interview guests who have created principled organizations, and we showcase authors, academics, consultants and business leaders who recognize that good business matters— to employees, to customers and to our planet.

Defining Good Business

Ethical, accountable, responsible, collaborative, service-oriented, vision-focused and *mission-based* are words that describe good business. In short, good business is principled business— business that recognizes there are foundational principles in life that cannot be violated without great consequence. One such principle is prosperity. All the world's great spiritual paths teach that as we give, we receive; yet few organizations design their business practices around this principle. Another universal principle is often referred to as the law of mind action—whatever we focus on increases; yet, if one were to follow a typical business leader around for a day, one would likely discover a much greater focus on problems than on solutions. Is it any wonder that organizational challenges appear to be increasing?

In our opinion good business is always vision-focused and mission-based, recognizing that that which we focus on (vision) becomes our reality; understanding that the purpose of the organization (mission) matters—to all its stakeholders. A good business is accountable, ethical, collaborative and service-oriented. The leaders of such a business know that they get what they give. We believe that at its core, good business is business that is grounded in universal spiritual principles.

Charles and Myrtle Fillmore were great role models. Charles Fillmore's career was in the railroad and real estate industries before he co-founded Unity, and Myrtle had been a schoolteacher. Here at Unity Village they created a good business based on universal spiritual principles and sound business practices. They were models of whole-brained leadership, demonstrating that it is possible to bring one's heart as well as one's head into the workplace. They used sound business practices while also providing opportunities for employees to develop spiritually. They were clearly committed to good business practices as well as transformational, spiritual ones. Charles' writings further demonstrate this commitment. In the first issue of *The Christian Business Man,* the earlier title of *Good Business* magazine, Charles wrote, "The financial world is ripe for the introduction of more successful methods of doing business. Cooperation, instead of competition, is the keynote of the new commercial wave that is sweeping over the land."[2] Today the waves of change are moving even faster. The world is ready for good business.

We have committed our careers to good business. We have collectively spent over 50 years leading and championing organizational change ... teaching, managing and modeling from a deep awareness of the unity of all of life. It has never made sense to us that people should leave their hearts at the front door when they arrive at work. It has never made sense to us that people should have to choose between living their deepest values and succeeding in their careers. It has never made sense to us that there should be an adversarial relationship between managers and their direct reports. It has never made sense to us that one should have to choose between money and meaning. We have long believed that businesses (and individuals) can do well financially while doing good works—for their customers, their employees and their communities.

We are so grateful to be alive at a time when more and more organizations are proving that what we have long taught is absolutely true. Organizations like the SAS Institute, Timberland Shoes, the Container Store, BioGenex, Tyson's Foods and Malden Mills are changing the fundamental nature of business, one decision at a time. You will read how they are doing so in this book.

Birthing *Good Business*

In order to create a book on good business we invited 20 of our first-year radio guests to write essays about what they believe to be the essence of good business. We trust that their stories, examples and advice will help you imagine what is possible for the world of work in general and for your experience of work in particular. We believe their examples offer new images of possibility for a more meaningful and sustainable way to "do" business. The primary purpose of this book is to stimulate more people—both managers and individual contributors—to think about what good business means to them and what their role is in creating a climate of good business in their organizations.

In Chapters 1 through 20 our guest authors weigh in on the question "What is the essence of good business?" Their contributions cover a wide range of perspectives. In Section I, Chapters 1 to 4 (Defining Good Business), you will read more about the foundational characteristics of good business from authors Brian Tracy, Daryl Conner, Corinne McLaughlin and Riane Eisler. In Section II, Chapters 5 to 11 (Soulful Leaders), Bil and Cher Holton, Richard Barrett, John Schuster, John Knowles, Stephen Blumberg, Peter Block and Margaret Wheatley share concrete suggestions for becoming a more soulful leader. Section III, Chapters 12 to 15 (Designing Enlightened Organizations), provides organizational change best practices. Susan Beck, Leigh Branham, Val Kinjerski, Margaret Benefiel and Debora Jackson share stories from the trenches as well as practical tools for changing your organization's culture. Section IV, Chapters 16 to 20 (Conscious Contributors), discusses what one person can do to create more meaningful work and a more successful career. Jim Bearden, Tom Hill, Ruth Ann Harnisch, Tricia Molloy and

Good Business

Judy Zerafa share ideas ranging from goal-setting, visualization and positive thinking to affirmations, accountability and
appreciation. In Section V, Chapters 21 and 22 (New Skills for
a New Millenium), we editors add our voices as authors by
sharing more of our own beliefs about good business as well
as the skills needed to create it.

At the end of the book there is a resource section that provides more information about Unity and its founders as well
as a sampling of articles from the early issues of *Good Business*
magazine. Though the articles' language and writing style
may seem a bit outdated and sexist, it is obvious that many of
the challenges facing businesspeople in the early 1930s are
the same as the ones we are facing at the end of the first
decade of the 21st century. In the resource section you will
also find a month's worth of daily good business affirmations
as well as ideas for forming a Good Business club in your
own organization, community or place of worship. These
resources are adapted from early issues of *Good Business* magazine.

Our personal goal for this book is that it will help transform the world by helping you transform your workplace.
Most adults spend a significant amount of their waking lives
at work. *Good Business* reminds us that we can live a meaningful life all the time—even in the workplace. It's simply a matter of choice!

Section I

Defining Good Business

1. Service and Satisfaction

Brian Tracy

Brian Tracy is chairman and CEO of Brian Tracy International, a company specializing in the training and development of individuals and organizations. He is the author of 47 books that have been published in 36 languages and has written, designed and produced more than 350 audio and video learning programs. For more information, visit *www.briantracy.com.*

Albert Einstein was once asked, "What is the purpose of human life?" He answered, somewhat surprised, "We are here to serve others; what other purpose could there be?" The most respected men and woman throughout history have been those who have dedicated their lives to serving other people in some way. A business is merely an organized way to serve people more efficiently and effectively than would be possible for an individual. A business is the way that people bring together the various resources of money, labor, raw materials, real estate and other facilities, to create products and services that enhance the lives of other people.

Peter Drucker, renowned management consultant, was once asked, "What is the purpose of a business?" He replied, "The purpose of a business is to create and keep a customer. The profits are the result of creating and keeping customers in a cost-effective way."

The true measure of business success is always customer satisfaction. The true measure of customer satisfaction is repeat business. The essence of good business is therefore simple: Good businesses are those that create products and services that people want, need and are willing to pay for—in a cost-effective way. As a result, these businesses satisfy their customers so much that their customers want to buy from them again—and bring their friends.

Good businesses, however, have an even greater depth and meaning than simply pleasing customers. Each person must earn their daily bread by doing something in the world. Each of us must "pay our dues." In exchange for food, clothing, accommodation, transportation and all other things that constitute the good life, each of us must make a contribution of some kind, in some way, that improves and enriches the lives or work of other people.

Aristotle asked the question, "How shall we live in order to be happy?" His conclusion was that the achievement of personal happiness was the ultimate end of all individual human activity. Everything that a person does in his/her daily life is aimed at somehow attaining happiness for that person. People are successful to the degree to which they are capable of achieving happiness consistently and predictably.

I — Defining Good Business

Here is a wonderful discovery: human beings are only happy when they are serving other people in some way. We are uniquely designed by God and nature to achieve our greatest sense of personal meaning and satisfaction when we know that what we are doing somehow enhances the life of someone else.

Successful businesspeople love their work. They look forward to every day. They get their greatest joy from knowing that they are making a difference in the lives of others. They believe in their products and services. They believe in their companies. They believe in their customers. And they believe in themselves and their ability to make an important contribution.

It has been said that "happiness is the progressive realization of a worthy ideal or goal." What this means is that we feel the happiest when we feel that we are making progress, hour by hour and day by day, toward the achievement of something significant and worthwhile to us.

It is not the destination that is as important as the journey itself. This is why the starting point of a successful business is the development of a step-by-step plan by which the business, and the people in it, are going to create and keep customers in a cost-effective way.

The essence of good business is when the business actually achieves the objectives that it has set out for itself in terms of sales, revenues, costs, people and net cash flow. The ability to "make your plan" is the true measure of the confidence and effectiveness of the businesspeople involved.

However, a business does not exist in a vacuum. Every business is in competition with every other comparable business that the customer might choose.

For this reason, good businesspeople develop an "obsession" with customer service. They think about their customers morning, noon and night. They think continually about how they can please and satisfy their customers better than anyone else. In striving for personal and business success, businesspeople are forced to focus outward on the customer and how they can most please their customers every single day.

The essence of good business therefore requires "continuous and never-ending improvement (CANEI)." There is a rule in business that says "whatever got you to where you are today is not enough to get you any further."

Successful businesspeople get their ultimate joy from pleasing their customers. But to achieve this joy and satisfaction, they must be continually improving everything they do so that their customers will voluntarily choose their products and services over those being offered by their competitors.

Many businesspeople tend to be scrupulously honest in everything they do, both internally and externally. Because business is based largely on the factor of trust, the most valuable asset of any business is its reputation. Reputation may be defined as "how you are known to your customers."

The most successful businesses and businesspeople have the very best reputations with their customers, their bankers, their employees and their suppliers. Trust in business acts as a lubricant that makes everything function more smoothly and efficiently. With high levels of trust, agreements and alterations to agreements can be made with a telephone call, e-mail or handshake. Lengthy, laborious and expensive contract revisions are seldom necessary.

Internally, good businesses treat their people very well, knowing that their people are the most important elements in taking care of their customers. Each year, studies are done to determine what constitutes "a great place to work." The 100 best companies to work for are written up annually as a reference source. In every case, the most important factor, from the point of view of the employees, is the element of trust that exists in the company. When employees are asked what they mean by the word *trust*, they say, "In this company, I feel that I can make a mistake without being criticized or punished."

W. Edwards Deming, the quality guru who advised Japanese industry after World War II and turned Japan into a high-quality industrial powerhouse, said that one of the most important things that a company does is to "drive out fear." Since fear represents the greatest obstacle to creativity and high performance, when businesses drive out fear, they create an environment where creativity and high performance are free to flourish.

The opposite of fear is love. There seems to be an element of love that runs through the thinking and the operations of successful businesses. Top businesspeople love their work. They love their products and services. They love their customers. They love their staff. They feel as if their business is a large family and everyone involved in the business is a family member.

In a good business, the top people are continuously looking for ways to express appreciation for each of their staff members. They seek out opportunities to give praise and approval for both large and small achievements. They hand out both tangible and intangible rewards, both money and opportunities for advancement. In a very positive way, top businesspeople look upon members of their staff very much as if they were their children, constantly seeking ways to encourage them and to help them develop their full potentials both as employees and as individuals.

Perhaps the most important word in successful business is *contribution*. The job of each person in a business is to make a valuable contribution and continually seek ways to increase the value of that contribution.

In life, our rewards will always be in direct proportion to the value of our service to others. As we increase our ability to serve others, by learning new skills or by working more efficiently, we increase our personal value and the additional rewards that we are likely to receive in the future.

One of the best questions you can ask each day is "What can I do to increase the value of my contribution to my company and my customers today?"

The best news is that this focus on customer service, on continually increasing your personal value and the value of your contribution, is a perfectly selfish act. The more you serve other people, and the better you serve them, the happier and more fulfilled you will feel inside. The ultimate is when you reach the point where you can "lose yourself" in service to others, sometimes losing track of time because you are so busy doing things that enrich the personal lives and work of your customers.

The essence of good business is simple: find a product or service that you really like and believe in, produce that product or service at the highest possible quality, continually get better, and then throw your whole heart into taking care of your customers in the very best way that you know how.

If you do these things regularly until they become as natural to you as breathing, not only will you be financially successful in business, but you will be respected and esteemed by all the people around you. You will have the great satisfaction of knowing that every day you are making a difference in the lives of other people. You will be living your life in such a way that you will be happy most of the time. And best of all, you will be fulfilling your God-given potential.

2. Corporate Social Responsibility: The Foundation of Good Business

Corinne McLaughlin

Corinne McLaughlin is executive director of the Center for Visionary Leadership in California and North Carolina, and co-author of *Spiritual Politics, Builders of the Dawn,* and *The Practical Visionary: A New World Guide to Spiritual Growth and Social Change.* She coordinated a national task force for President Clinton's Council on Sustainable Development and taught politics at American University. She is a Fellow of the World Business Academy and the Findhorn Foundation, and is also co-founder of Sirius Community, a spiritual/environmental center in Massachusetts. She can be reached at *corinnemc@visionarylead.org* or at *www.visionarylead.org.*

Is your company a good business? A good business strives to create good relationships—not only with customers and shareholders, but also with employees, suppliers, the local community and the natural environment. Fundamentally, good business is a spiritual approach to business. It takes a whole-systems view that consciously balances the needs of all the many stakeholders in a company.

What does spirituality in business mean to you? Is it being guided by an inner moral compass and embodying personal values of honesty, integrity and fairness while doing good quality work? Is it treating co-workers and employees well? Is it participating in spiritual study groups, or using prayer, meditation or intuitive guidance at work? Or is it making your business socially responsible in how it affects the environment, serves the community, or helps create a better world? All of these expressions of spirituality in business are embraced by thousands of businesspeople across the country.

People increasingly want to bring a greater sense of meaning and purpose into their work life. They want their work to reflect their personal mission in life. Many companies are finding the most effective way to bring spiritual values into the workplace is to clarify the company's vision and mission and to align it with a higher purpose and a deeper commitment to serve both customers and the community.

Growing numbers of people want their spirituality to be more than just faith and belief—they want it to be practical and applied. They want to bring their whole selves to work: body, mind and spirit. Many people are finding that they can actually strengthen the bottom line—profit—by embodying their values. They've discovered they can "do well by doing good."

People are finding there's more to life—and business—than profit alone. Money as the single bottom line is increasingly a thing of the past. In a post-Enron, post-Madoff world, values and ethics are an urgent concern. Over the past decade, pressure on businesses from socially responsible investors and consumers, as well as shareholder activists, has pushed them to consider a "triple bottom line": people, planet, profit. This is a rapidly growing trend creating more transparency and accountability in how companies treat their employees, their community and the environment.

Author Patricia Aburdene calls this trend "conscious capitalism" or "stakeholder capitalism," and names it as an emerging "megatrend" in her book *Megatrends 2010*. She notes that socially responsible corporations tend to be well-managed, and she suggests that great management is the best way to predict superior financial performance. Companies that have made real changes and retooled to be more energy efficient have been able to weather the economic downturn better than their competitors. And to the surprise of many, the movement for spirituality in business is beginning to transform corporate America from the inside out.

Applying spirituality in the work environment is more acceptable than religion, as it's more generic and inclusive. Instead of emphasizing belief and dogma as religion does, spirituality emphasizes how ethical values are applied and embodied. For example, the Container Store nationwide tells workers they are "morally obligated to help customers solve problems."[1] The CEO of Vermont Country Store, a popular national catalogue company, honored an employee who told the truth about a company problem in a widely circulated memo—rather than firing him. This greatly increased morale and built a sense of trust in the company.

Are spirituality and profitability mutually exclusive? Recent research shows that bringing ethics and spirituality into the workplace can lead to increased productivity and profitability as well as employee retention, enhanced morale, customer loyalty and brand reputation.

A study done at the University of Chicago by Professor Curtis Verschoor found that companies with a defined corporate commitment to ethical principles do better financially than companies that don't make ethics a key management component.[2] Research by McKinsey and Co. Australia shows that when companies engage in programs that use spiritual techniques for their employees, productivity improves and turnover is greatly reduced.[3]

A report released by Goldman Sachs, one of the world's leading investment banks, showed that companies in six major sectors (energy, mining, steel, food, beverages and media) that are considered leaders in implementing environmental, social and governance policies have outperformed the general stock market by 25 percent since August 2005. In addition, 72 percent of these companies have outperformed their peers over the same period.[4] Public shaming of companies, such as Nike when it used overseas sweatshops, led to major drops in earnings until such companies worked to improve conditions.

Good Business

In today's highly competitive environment, the most talented people seek out organizations that reflect their inner values and provide opportunities for personal development and community service, not just bigger salaries. Unlike the marketplace economy of 20 years ago, today's information- and service-dominated economy requires instantaneous decision-making and better relationships with customers and employees.

Many businesspeople use prayer at work: for guidance in decision-making, to prepare for difficult situations, when they are going through a tough time, or to give thanks for something good. Timberland Shoes CEO Jeffrey B. Swartz talks openly about using his prayer book and religious beliefs to guide business decisions and company policy, often consulting his rabbi. Kris Kalra, CEO of BioGenex, uses the Hindu holy text the Bhagavad Gita to steer his business out of trouble.

Meditation classes have been held over the years at many major corporations, such as Medtronic, Apple, Google, Yahoo, McKinsey, IBM, Hughes Aircraft, Cisco and Raytheon, because these classes often improve productivity and creativity and create more harmony in the workplace. Greystone Bakery in upstate New York has a period of meditative silence before meetings begin so people can get in touch with their inner selves and focus on the issues to be discussed.

Executives at Xerox have gone on weeklong retreats led by Marlowe Hotchkiss of the Ojai Foundation to learn a Native American model of council meetings and experience vision quests. A vision quest inspired one manager with the idea to create one of Xerox's hottest sellers, a 97 percent recyclable machine.[5]

Some companies use spiritual affirmations to strengthen employee morale. Marriott hotels often place signs with inspirational affirmations in staff hallways to create a positive atmosphere. Other companies have spiritual study groups initiated by staff.

ABC Evening News reported that the American Stock Exchange has a Torah study group; Boeing has Christian, Jewish and Muslim prayer groups; and Microsoft has an online prayer service.[6] Spiritual study groups in some companies are sometimes called "Higher Power Lunches"—instead of the usual "power lunches."

Corporations are increasingly hiring chaplains to support their employees, as they are good listeners and quick responders in crises, and they can serve people of any or no faith. *U.S. News and World Report* estimates there are more than 4,000 chaplains nationwide.[7] Tyson's Foods, for example, has more than 125 part-time chaplains in the U.S., Canada and Mexico.[8] Fast-food companies such as Taco Bell and Pizza Hut hire chaplains from many faiths to minister to employees with problems and credit the chaplains with reducing turnover rates by half.

Increasingly, businesspeople find that the key area for applying spirituality is employee relationships. Southwest Airlines, for example, says that people are its most important resource, and company policy is to treat employees like family, knowing that if they are treated well, they in turn will treat customers well.

Aaron Feuerstein, CEO of Malden Mills in Lawrence, Massachusetts, which produces popular Polartec fabrics, believes that people are the best asset a company has. He says a company has an equal responsibility to its community and to itself. Since his town has high unemployment, he kept all 3,000 employees on his payroll after a major fire destroyed three out of its four factory buildings several years ago. Feuerstein told me in an interview that his workers repaid his generosity by helping him rebuild, resulting in a 25 percent increase in productivity and a 66 percent drop in quality defects.

The late Anita Roddick, founder of the Body Shop, with stores all over the world, purposely built a soap factory near Glasgow, Scotland, because it was an area of high unemployment, urban decay and demoralization. She made a moral decision to employ the unemployable and put 25 percent of the net profits back into the community because she said this is what keeps the soul of the company alive. Timberland, the popular New Hampshire-based shoe company, pays employees for 40 hours of volunteer work annually, and many companies increasingly support volunteer work by employees.[9]

Tom Chappell, CEO of Tom's of Maine, which produces soaps and toothpastes, gives away 10 percent of its pretax profits to charities. Tom's gives employees four paid hours a month to volunteer for community service and uses all-natural ingredients because they are good for the environment. After studying at Harvard Divinity School, Chappell re-engineered his business into a sort of ministry, saying that he is ministering—but doing it in the marketplace, not in the church, because he understands the marketplace better than the church.

Many companies are using more environmentally sustainable practices as a way to express their spiritual values. By reducing, reusing and recycling, Fetzer Wine has reduced its garbage by 95 percent since 1990, according to the company's Web site. Fetzer uses 100 percent renewable (green) energy and has switched from petroleum to biodiesel fuel, while farming its own grapes organically.

Whole Foods, the world's leading natural and organic foods supermarket, made the largest renewable energy purchase anywhere to offset 100 percent of its electricity use in all 180 stores. It is purchasing more than 458,000 megawatt-hours of renewable energy credits from wind farms—the same environmental impact of taking 60,000 cars off the road or planting 90,000 acres of trees.[10]

A major effort to support good businesses is the socially responsible investment (SRI) movement. More and more people want to invest in companies that embody values they care about—social, environmental, ethical—and this trend will grow exponentially in future years. By early 2009, socially responsible investing had become a $2.7 trillion industry, growing 40 percent faster than the overall fund universe, according to the Social Investment Forum. My husband, Gordon Davidson, was one of the first executive directors of the Forum when it started in 1987, and he would often field questions from major media such as *The Wall Street Journal*, who were skeptical until they saw the stellar financial performance of socially responsible companies.

Social investment includes four strategies: screening, shareholder advocacy, community investing and socially responsible venture capital. Screening stocks to a set of "screens" or criteria involves asking, for example, "Does the company pollute the environment, violate fair labor practices, promote women and minorities, display integrity in advertising?" Many SRI funds, such as Calvert, avoid companies that produce firearms, nuclear power, tobacco or alcohol.

Shareholder advocacy is another powerful SRI strategy in which shareholders have pressured major corporations such as McDonald's and J.C. Penney to be more socially responsible through shareholder resolutions and divestment campaigns.

Community investing is a third strategy that encourages people to invest in valuable local projects that might not qualify for funding, such as buying abandoned, deteriorating buildings and rehabbing them for poor people, thus creating good jobs and safe neighborhoods as ShoreBank of Chicago does.

Socially responsible venture capital is the fourth SRI strategy, as socially conscious capital is key for getting new start-up businesses with a social mission up and running. Capital Missions and the Investors' Circle are two effective examples of this approach. Information on social investing can be found at the Social Investment Forum: *www.socialinvest.org*.

Information on socially responsible companies can be found at Ethical Markets: *www.ethicalmarkets.com*.

There is also a growing movement of "social entrepreneurs," who create "social benefit corporations"—for-profit companies created primarily for a social mission. They are blurring the lines between for-profit and nonprofit approaches. D.light, for example, has a mission of replacing millions of polluting and dangerous kerosene lamps in the developing world with solar-powered lamps. The founder, Sam Goldman, a former Peace Corps volunteer, wanted to help poor people in Benin, where he had served, and he discovered that a business model fueled by profit could distribute the lamps more quickly and efficiently and fulfill his social mission better than a nonprofit organization.

Today there are new financial indexes that track the performance of socially responsible companies. The leading benchmark for socially and environmentally responsible investing worldwide is the KLD Domini 400 Social Index. The Dow Jones Dharma Global Index tracks companies aligned with the principles of nonviolence and Earth stewardship.

The movements for social investment, socially responsible business, environmentally sustainable business, and Spirit in business are all hopeful signs that business, as the most powerful institution in the world today, may be transforming from within. What is emerging is a new attitude towards the workplace as a place to fulfill a deeper purpose, both personally and organizationally.

Are you already part of this growing movement, or would you like to contribute in some way as an owner, worker, investor and/or consumer? There are some easy ways to begin. For example, you could make a commitment to tell three people in your workplace something that you appreciate about them. Or make a commitment to express gratitude to your co-workers more directly in the next week. You could also make a commitment to tell the truth more regularly. And you could meditate on a business decision and ask for spiritual guidance.

You could create better relationships at work by actively listening to your co-workers: listen carefully to what someone says, especially if there's a conflict, and then feed back what you hear the person saying, and ask if you've understood him/her correctly. You could also invite your co-workers to a brown bag lunch where you discuss spirituality in your workplace, and ask each person what it means to him or her and how each might bring more of their spiritual values to work. Posting inspirational messages or pictures in your workplace is another way to bring your spiritual values to work. Or you could organize a recycling initiative at your company or a campaign to reduce wasted energy and so help protect the environment.

Most important, you can become a more conscious consumer/investor by striving to create coherence between your values and how you spend and invest your money, thus supporting socially responsible businesses.

Each day, more and more businesses are helping to create a better world by being more socially responsible in how they treat people and the environment. They are proving that spirituality helps, rather than harms, the bottom line. As Kahlil Gibran reminds us in The Prophet, "Work is love made visible."[11]

3. Spiritual Wholeness: Operationalizing the Intangible
Daryl Conner

Daryl R. Conner is chairman and co-founder of Conner Partners®, an Atlanta-based consulting firm that specializes in strategy execution. He is an internationally recognized leader in organizational change and serves as an advisor and mentor to senior executives around the globe. In more than 35 years of practice, Daryl has worked with many of the most successful organizations in the world, including Fortune 500 companies, government agencies and nonprofit institutions, to help them achieve the full intent of their most urgent and important initiatives. A dynamic public speaker, he has addressed thousands of executives in corporate settings, national conferences and public programs. Daryl has authored two books—*Managing at the Speed of Change* (Random House, 1993) and *Leading at the Edge of Chaos* (John Wiley & Sons, 1998)—and more than 250 publications, including journal and magazine articles, monographs, book chapters and videos.

Let's start with the concept of "business" (good or otherwise). Most people relate to the term as referring to for-profit enterprises; however, similar dynamics occur in non-profit concerns as well. From my perspective, business refers to the exchange of products or services for some type of compensation, which may take the form of a wide range of currencies (wages/fees in most for-profit entities, and other outcomes—such as the possibility of the betterment of humanity—for nonprofit institutions).

As to conducting business in a "good" manner, I see the actual operation of an enterprise as judgment neutral in the same way that a baseball game is not inherently positive or negative. From a purely objective standpoint, the results, and the processes for getting there, are what they are. True, this doesn't stop most people from forming and expressing opinions about both the process and outcome based on their frame of reference (e.g., "I don't like the way the coach changed the batting lineup," "I won a bundle on the game Sunday"). However, the verdict declared about the degree to which a business is "good" says more about the biases of the person rendering the opinion than about the judgment-neutral business events themselves.

Reframing the Question

Because the use of "good" (and its assumed counterpart, "bad") to frame the question at hand could imply a level of judgment that I'd rather avoid, I favor replacing "good" with "wholeness" and frame the presenting question as "What is the essence of operating a business from a wholeness perspective?" Once I've explored this way of looking at the issues, I'll return to the wording of the original question to offer an answer.

I would like to start by describing a scale that positions the operation of a business somewhere on a range from a wholeness mindset at one extreme to a segmentation mindset at the other end. Using these distinctions as the reference points isn't a mere play on words. The terms good and bad are loaded with all kinds of implications for most people (not the least of which is a general implication of a mutual exclusiveness—one worthy and the other dreadful; one right, the other wrong; one to be exalted, the other eliminated).

Exploring the question through the lens of wholeness and segmentation offers a different perspective. These two terms are not mutually exclusive, nor is one "right" while the other is "wrong." There are times when segmentation is not only acceptable but is the preferable way to move a business forward—for instance, separating work into different tasks or geographic areas can have some real advantages. On the other hand, segmentation taken too far or applied ineffectively can create silo thinking, territoriality and warlord mentality at the organizational level and a sense of fragmentation and alienation at the personal level.

Synergy and Wholeness

Operating a business from a wholeness perspective reflects a bias for synergy (from the Greek root *syn*, meaning "together," and *ergo*, meaning "to work"). A synergistic environment is one in which cooperative action among the parts results in a total effect greater than the sum of what each element could have produced independently. For such outcomes to take place among the distinct parts, they must also function from wholeness.

Sustainable strength, effectiveness and efficiency come from unifying the various aspects of an organization in a synergistic manner. This is true for a business's human assets as well as its financial, technological or brick-and-mortar assets. While divergence and compartmentalization are sometimes needed, they should be applied with the ultimate aim of forming some degree of coherent unification.

Specific to this writing, I intend to advocate that when it comes to running a business, unity is a healthier, stronger and more productive force than separation. Wholeness is not only more intellectually, emotionally and spiritually appealing than segmentation, it is a more effective paradigm for competing in the marketplace.

Beyond Profitability

A second thread I would like to weave into the discussion is the notion that business goals can and should go beyond profitability to include higher aspirations. Evidence is beginning to surface that supports this as a viable approach to achieving bottom-line results. In the groundbreaking book *Firms of Endearment*, the authors identified companies that financially outperformed the S&P 500 by a wide margin but were also characterized as operating within a "conscious capitalism" framework. These companies were as competitive as any in a free-market economy, but they functioned with a "humanistic soul." They strived for profits but did so in a way that maximized value for all stakeholders—not only investors and partners, but customers, employees and society itself. "They are the ultimate value creators: They create emotional value, experiential value, social value, and of course, financial value. People who interact with such companies feel safe, secure and pleased in their dealings. They enjoy working with or for the company, buying from it, investing in it, and having it as a neighbor."[1]

The authors further declare that conscious capitalism is no passing fad. "The search for meaning is changing expectations in the marketplace and in the workplace. Indeed, we believe it is changing the very soul of capitalism."[2] At the heart of this perspective is running a business with goals that include, but aren't limited to, profitability. The paradox is that those companies that focused on more than making money made more money than those that focused exclusively on making money. The message here is that it can be both fulfilling and profitable to include higher-order aspirations in a business model.

Wholeness and Spiritual Pursuits

There are many worthy "higher order" goals a company could aspire to (environmental sustainability, reducing world hunger, caring for the homeless, etc.), which could be directly tied to an organization's products and services (e.g., a company that produces solar power) or funded from revenue generated in unrelated ways (a manufacturing company pledging a percent of its annual profits to a homeless shelter). What I want to explore here is the integration of spirituality into the workplace—the explicit goal of incorporating multiple, diverse spiritual pursuits as part of a business's operating model.

It is possible and important to reduce dramatically the number of artificial boundaries separating work and one's spiritual pursuit. Professional activities take up an enormous amount of a person's available time and energy. To partition life into discrete work-centered versus spirit-centered compartments not only negates the synergistic impact each can have on the other, it denies a person the opportunity to live a fully integrated existence. How can people stand with integrity for who they are if fundamental aspects of their being are only allowed to surface under certain circumstances?

From a wholeness standpoint, it is important that people bring their full selves to the work environment, including their spiritual preferences. Mitroff and Denton's landmark 1999 study of spirituality in the workplace found that people do not want to compartmentalize or fragment their lives. Rather, their search for meaning, purpose and wholeness is an integrated and ongoing task. To confine this search to one day a week or "after hours" violates their sense of wholeness. Soul is not something one can leave at home.[3]

Of course, not everyone partakes in matters of a spiritual nature, and many who do have little enthusiasm for reflecting that side of themselves where they work. Why do some people assimilate spirituality into their day-to-day work activities while others separate that portion of their lives from their work? This is an intriguing question, but pondering it only raises more questions that beg equal attention:

- What contributes to many people feeling they are expected to limit, if not eliminate, any expression at work of what they consider sacred?

- Why do so many organizations fail to see the connection between employees who aspire to make a difference and the business that aspires to make money?

- What would it take for people to feel comfortable bringing their whole selves to work, including whatever spiritual path they adhere to?

- Is it possible for people to overtly live out their spiritual values at work without it hampering productivity or becoming intrusive to others?

- How can people openly reflect their faith without it appearing as proselytizing?

- How could a person's spiritual pursuits produce value for customers and the employer?

- Is it possible to create a work environment that not only allows for, but also encourages, the open expression of different faiths while ensuring each is respected and honored?

- How can the integration of spirituality enhance cohesion among colleagues and increase productivity?

- How can organizations go beyond "accepting" spirituality in the work setting and truly embed it into the business models they use?

Wholeness and Meaning

Questions of this nature are more than just interesting to me. They represent an important but typically ignored component in the formula for a successful business: "meaning." Over the last three decades, I have observed a shift in the consciousness of both the workforce and customer constituencies. A key part of this recalibration appears to be a much higher value now being placed on the search for meaning in one's life. Spiritual pursuits are not the only way to find meaning, but for many people, being engaged in some type of spiritual journey is what leads them to an enhanced sense of purpose in their lives.

To an increasing extent, people who are part of this consciousness shift appear far less willing to fragment their lives than in the past. They expect their quest for meaning should be able to cross what have traditionally been impassable boundaries. They are no longer willing to confine their introspective exploration to a church, synagogue or temple. Segmentation like this is seen as infringing on their desire to live lives that are more integrated, and they resist anything that inhibits them being all of who they are, regardless of the setting. The individuals I have monitored want to live seamless lives—whether in prayer or deep meditation, watching a movie, cutting the grass, or showing up for work.

Along with this flourishing interest in spiritual expression at work is a related trend—people want this freedom without having to limit themselves to places of work composed solely or primarily of people who subscribe to a single religion. More and more, people are seeking work environments where all expressions of spirituality are welcomed.

This means people are searching for employment where they feel their sacred aims will be more than merely tolerated by management and colleagues who hold to other faiths. They want the confidence of knowing their spiritual journey will be treated with the same dignity afforded others. They want their path acknowledged as one of many heartfelt routes in which a Divine connection can be achieved and assurance that it will not be imposed on, disrespected or discounted in any way.

What Would It Look Like?

From a unity (versus separation) standpoint, there are three aspects to a successful business:

What We Do is the content of the work done—what's involved (tools, methods, procedures and processes, etc.) in developing and delivering the products and services provided customers.

Who We Are is the substance of what the people within a business have to offer as humans—their composition of "beingness," the quality of their interaction, and the frame of mind they bring to life as expressed through their work.

How We Prosper is the economic engine that drives a business. Key influences are things like the customer value proposition, the financial model for ensuring profitability, and how the enterprise is structured and operated to optimize efficiency and effectiveness.

The work that is done (what we do), applied through a strong sense of character (who we are) within a well-managed, profitable structure (how we prosper), is at the heart of what successful, wholeness-oriented businesses are about. These are not three discrete elements; they are interdependent, intertwining threads in the fabric of how a business achieves its desired outcomes. For synergy to flourish, they must be combined so their effect is exponentially greater than their individual contributions. The result serves as the foundation of an emerging business model—one that synthesizes being an ambitious, competitive enterprise that is well structured and orchestrated with having a strong spiritual center of gravity.

Although all three elements are essential to operating a business from a wholeness perspective, the rest of this essay focuses solely on the who-we-are thread, not because it's more important than the other two, but because it represents less familiar territory for most people and therefore is more neglected. Many businesses are less wholeness-oriented than they otherwise could be simply because of inattention to the who-we-are aspect of their operation.

Who We Are

Each wholeness-based organization must determine how best to manifest its who-we-are aspirations. ("By what character traits do we want to individually and collectively define ourselves and how will we make progress towards those standards?") No two efforts of this nature are the same, yet the direction and tone of any such endeavor have a distinctive quality about it. Attributes like clarity of vision, commitment to honesty, devotion to providing value, passion for the work, and the quality of customer/employee relationships are representative of what clarifying who we are is about.

Another characteristic central to who we are in organizations seeking to integrate a spiritual perspective into the workplace is the belief that there is an underlying purpose that gives our lives meaning and shapes the way they unfold. There are many ways to interpret the source of this power (God, the single source of creation, the ultimate intelligence, the Divine, etc.). Regardless of how people relate to this source, two things are important from an organizational perspective:

- A conviction that each person tied to the business (colleagues and customers) plays a unique role in a greater picture than can be fully comprehended.

- A commitment to encouraging people at all levels of an organization to explore what it means to integrate their spiritual beliefs into what they and the business are trying to accomplish.

Finally, key to the integration of who we are into the work environment is the ability to operationalize the intangible—that is, to create a functional link between each individual's spiritual beliefs and the day-to-day activities associated with the individual's work. This calls for finding practical ways in which each individual's connection to a larger purpose can have a constructive, pragmatic, business-related impact on customer and colleague relationships.

One particularly valuable approach to creating an enterprise that integrates who we are into its business model is to formulate a statement or list of declarations everyone in the company can support as a collective way of expressing their individual faith's guidance. Such a statement provides a context (framework and language) that helps people apply their company's who-we-are perspectives to day-to-day realities while remaining aligned with and supportive of the various spiritual directions they each represent. It can also create opportunities for people to learn more about and from each other, appreciate the diversity that exists among their various spiritual orientations, and identify common ground where their individual dispositions reflect similarities.

AN EXAMPLE

The description that follows is how one for-profit organization (referred to here as WholeCo) articulated its desire to integrate a sense of spirituality into its professional environment. It is not offered as the way for a business to approach such an undertaking, but rather is intended to be representative of how challenges of this nature can be framed and pursued.

WholeCo created a statement to describe its spiritual aspirations to current employees and prospective recruits. Employees refer to it on a frequent basis to stay centered on the kind of work environment they hope to foster. It is also used with recruits to establish clear expectations about the company's who-we-are intentions. The full document includes several components—presented here are only two:

- How can we operationalize the intangible at WholeCo?
- Why are we here at WholeCo?

How can we operationalize the intangible at WholeCo?

There are five key statements related to operationalizing the intangible at WholeCo:

1. It comes through us but not from us.

When pursuing our work, we use our intellect, rely on our perceptions, apply our judgment, and engage our various techniques, but what we have learned to depend on the most isn't actually ours to own. What happens when we're at our best comes not from us but through us. Our potential as a firm can unfold only when we tap into a much deeper reservoir than we, individually and collectively, can take credit for. When clients and employees receive their greatest value from us, we are the conduit, not the source, of what happens.

2. Being here is not an accident.

We are in this place at this time for a reason. We don't believe that people join our company or that clients engage us by accident or through coincidence. As we see it, we each travel within a particular current that brings us into contact with the very people, situations and circumstances that enable us to learn the lessons waiting for us and use them as a catalyst for growth. Our task is to remain as centered as possible on our individual and collective purposes, and to help each other and clients who are attempting to do the same. This is accomplished by pushing as hard as possible toward new horizons while at the same time accepting wherever our flow takes us. We get into trouble when we decide our egos know more about what's best for us rather than allow ourselves to follow the natural flow of the Divine guidance we're offered.

3. We are not in control, yet we are accountable for our choices.

Because we are subject to forces outside ourselves, it is an illusion to think we can control all aspects of what happens to us, much less to our clients. At the same time, we believe we are accountable for what takes place in our lives and the lives of those we influence. We are part of a universal dance—a grand design—yet we influence our own destinies.

4. We are all connected.

As we each pursue our own paths, underneath what appears as our separateness is a connection that actually bonds us all as one. We may be distinct waves, but we're all part of a much larger ocean. It's in our individual and collective best interest to treat clients and each other with this in mind. What we do or fail to do for someone else is in some fundamental way the same as doing it—or failing to do it—for ourselves.

5. We share the same journey.

Sometimes it's easy to focus on how different we are from our clients or each other, but it's best to remember that, in the ultimate sense, we're all equals when it comes to finding our way in life. None of us has all the answers and we all get lost occasionally, so understanding and compassion are essential to helping each other as best we can.

These five statements are not meant to be an inclusive list of all the common ground shared by those in our company. These are but examples to demonstrate our belief that it's possible to "operationalize the intangible" in a business setting. Far from seeing the pursuit of a spiritual path as unrelated to business, we see it as an integral part of our commercial model. We are committed to being an organization where people are actively engaged in internal journeys of this nature and are encouraged to integrate this aspect of their lives into the character of our firm.

Why are we here at WholeCo?

We are here to serve.

There are four main constituents we believe we are meant to serve. In rank order they are: ourselves, our culture, our clients and our communities. Listing ourselves and the firm before customers is an intentional declaration of priority that requires explanation.

Every time a flight crew prepares passengers for takeoff, they remind the adults that in case of an unexpected drop in cabin pressure, they are to put the oxygen masks on themselves first before attending to their children. It is an important reminder because as a parent, one's instinct is to do exactly the opposite. In a crisis, the majority of people will automatically take care of their children before thinking of themselves. Although this may conform to a common stereotype of the kind of self-sacrifice a mother or father should display, statistics prove that parents actually provide better care for their children during an emergency if they first ensure they won't lose consciousness themselves.

The message is very clear ... you can't properly attend to others unless you first take care of yourself.

We wholeheartedly concur with this view. Unless those of us within our organization are physically, emotionally and spiritually healthy, we will be unprepared to bring the intended value to our clients. Likewise, unless our organization creates a strong, supportive yet challenging culture from which our people operate, clients will not receive the promised benefits from our collective experience and knowledge. It then follows that contributing to the communities where we conduct business is only possible if our clients have been adequately attended to and our company has profits we can allocate for this purpose.

This means all four of our primary constituencies are important, but there is a preferred sequence in terms of where and when emphasis is placed on attending to needs. Healthy employees are a prerequisite for a healthy organization, which is a prerequisite for healthy clients, which is a prerequisite for healthy communities.

Serving Ourselves

In this context, serving ourselves means taking care of our respective needs. At WholeCo, this is accomplished in three ways:

We nurture and safeguard whatever is at the core of our lives.

In a fast-paced, demanding environment like ours, it is easy to succumb to the various pressures and lose sight of what is in our long-term best interest. It is essential that each of us know what physical, emotional, family and spiritual requirements we have for remaining whole, healthy and vibrant. We must then make decisions and take actions that are consistent with fulfilling these requirements. Even though our leadership takes a strong stance on helping people take care of themselves first, it is ultimately the responsibility of each of us to ensure we nourish and protect our beingness in both the personal and professional aspects of our lives.

We tend to the lessons we are here to learn.

We should always seek the deeper truth in whatever happens and search for the knowledge or wisdom it has to offer. There are as many answers to the question "Why am I here?" as there are people in our company. We believe an individual's ultimate reason for being at WholeCo goes beyond deliverables, utilization rates or performance reviews. Why each of us is here is as close to the heart and as embedded in the soul as one can get in a business environment.

At some point while employed with our company, most people wrestle with some tough questions: What is to be accomplished at the most personal level by me being part of this organization? Am I here to strengthen and apply a unique gift I've been blessed with? Am I here to face fears I've previously avoided? Am I here to provide value to many people (clients, colleagues and others) over an extended time, or might my primary purpose be to help only one person successfully encounter a single crucial circumstance in his or her life? Is my part to soar to new heights, or is it to experience a humbling fall and learn from it what's needed to become stronger? Is the focus for my being here my work within the company and/or the clients we serve, or am I here to draw strength from the people in WholeCo who support me in a calling that lies elsewhere? Is my journey a combination of some or all of these?

There is no single answer to these questions, and there is no fixed timeline for resolving them. Each person must engage them at his or her own pace and in his or her own way.

We search for an understanding regarding our purpose.

Some people come to WholeCo with clarity about their purpose in life. Others appear to gain an understanding of their purpose only after facing some critical choices. Still others look back on what has taken place to find that purpose has been unfolding without their awareness. Whether we are graced with it from the beginning or it is discovered through difficult self-exploration, it is only when we understand and accept the higher design we are here to accomplish that we can accelerate our progress in that direction.

Whenever this clarity of purpose emerges, few of us are fully prepared for all the implications that come with it. In fact, most of us who work here report feeling humbled (if not overwhelmed at times) by the personal undertakings we are here to carry out. Fortunately, staying mindful of who we are offers many opportunities to learn the lessons critical to fulfilling our purpose. Without a bearing for guidance and a compass for steering, one is likely to view his or her work experience as unproductive at best and a source of disillusionment at worst. However, for those who are able to identify and draw on a clear sense of purpose, the personal, professional and spiritual rewards to be gained while working at WholeCo are substantial.

Serving the Culture

Strong professionals must be supported by a strong organizational culture. The culture inside WholeCo provides the clarity of values and behavioral guidance we feel is necessary to stay true to what we want to accomplish (personally and as a firm) and how we want to go about doing it.

We serve and strengthen our culture in two ways:

We focus on the culture itself.

We believe everyone in our company (leadership as well as line and support staff) has a responsibility to ensure that we maintain the cultural foundation needed to operate in a manner consistent with the challenging goals we have set for ourselves. A culture like ours does not materialize on its own. It requires considerable vigilance and dedication. Completing tasks in an effective, efficient and pleasant manner; promoting a synergistic atmosphere; establishing and fulfilling commitments appropriately; being courageous and disciplined in our actions; honoring and respecting each other's spiritual journeys; and continuing to renew our understanding of and commitment to who we are represent a few examples of what is needed to sustain our culture.

We attend to each other's needs within the organization.

How we serve one another is as critical as our service to clients; in some ways, it goes even deeper. As previously stated, it is up to each individual to determine why he or she came to WholeCo. Whatever that purpose is, we believe the rest of us are here to support that outcome. In other words, part of what everyone is here to do is to help others achieve what they are trying to accomplish (professionally, spiritually, etc.). Joining this company means integrating ourselves into an interdependent network of overlapping purpose-driven agendas.

From the time someone new comes on board, we each play some part in fulfilling that person's purpose for being here. We do this in many ways, but one of the more important is by holding each other accountable for meeting the who-we-are standards. It would be impossible to sustain our professional-spiritual quest without the love, compassion and support we provide each other. Maintaining the journey would also be impossible, however, without definitive criteria, tough feedback and consequences. The very lesson standing between a person and his or her goals might be a broken agreement someone fails to mention or poor quality on a deliverable that slips by without a word of feedback. We recognize and celebrate our victories, but we also care enough about each other to consistently and firmly hold one another to the standards that set us apart from other companies.

Serving Our Clients

With strong, healthy individuals and a solid cultural base to operate from, we are in a good position to serve our clients.

On the face of it, our primary value to clients is the service we provide. We take this responsibility seriously and do all we can to ensure that we live up to the confidence they place in us and the professional standards and expectations we have for ourselves.

We believe, however, that when we're engaged with clients, there is more taking place than a commercially defined relationship. Whether we can always see it or not, we believe there is a deeper purpose underlying our contractual obligations. We are playing a part in our clients' lives that goes beyond the formal boundaries of our work. Maybe our call is to be nothing more than an unusually honest and caring person with the necessary skills to address their needs, or maybe it's to unlock some long-standing issue in their lives. Maybe our gift is to serve as an inspirational model for them to admire and possibly emulate, or maybe it is simply not rejecting them at a personal level when they display dysfunctional behavior. Maybe we are there to be highly visible assets, or maybe we are there only to have a subtle influence from the shadows.

We may not always be aware of what the deeper purpose is, but we're confident one exists. For this reason, we need to treat each client interaction as an opportunity to fulfill that purpose. We have been brought into their lives and they into ours so something can happen that is in everyone's best interest. It is our job to remain open to what that is and to be a conduit for its fulfillment.

Serving Our Communities

Professionals who nurture and protect the core of their being, operate out of a healthy culture, and provide significant benefits to their customers are positioned to share the prosperity that such value generation creates. With personal, professional and organizational success comes a responsibility to serve beyond our clients and ourselves. We believe we are also here to serve the communities where we live and work, as well as the larger human community of which we are a part. Gratitude for what we have; compassion for those who are less fortunate; responsibility toward self, others and God; and a sense of stewardship for the resources we have to share (time, money and talents) dictate that we do nothing less. Together these motivations lead us to contribute to and strengthen the larger human pursuit, and to act on what is in our heads and hearts about "the right thing to do."

This kind of sharing can be accomplished at a personal level in the form of tithing, charitable contributions, volunteering, etc., or it can be attained in a collective manner by combining resources with others to achieve a greater impact than is possible through individual efforts. WholeCo seeks to address the latter through our Community Investment Program. (A separate document describes in detail how WholeCo contributes money and donates time to the communities where we conduct business.)

The above excerpt is from WholeCo's statement of "who we are." This is one particular company's effort at operationalizing the intangible. It should be seen only as an illustration of what can be done. Any organization hoping to incorporate a spiritual dimension into its work environment must uncover and invoke its own journey. One business cannot borrow another's way of articulating the common ground needed so people from all faiths can integrate their respective beliefs and practices into the core of their enterprise's business model. It is my hope in sharing this example that it might prompt the reader to open a dialogue in his or her organization regarding what might be included in the organization's version of "who we are."

The Essence

Let's revisit the original question: What is the essence of good business? Answer: At its crux, it is an enterprise generating a wake of positive influence on all the constituencies it touches. One of the contributing factors in making this happen is a work environment that fosters spiritual integration into its day-to-day operations. Key terms and phrases that resonate with this view of good business are unity, operationalizing the intangible, meaning, synergy and wholeness.

After reading this essay, if the challenge I've described doesn't sound formidable, I have failed in my mission. If the description of seeking unity through integrating spirituality into the workplace appears somewhat overwhelming, imagine trying to live up to what it calls for on a daily basis. Yet operationalizing the intangible isn't about trying to achieve perfection. It is about what happens when people decide that engaging in meaningful work is vitally important to them, yet they are challenged by the limitations of the human experience. They will catch themselves when they inevitably fall short of their synergistic goals, take steps to close all the gaps they can, and celebrate the times they are able to experience their aspirations. Operationalizing the intangible means having the courage to face the true price for being who we are and demonstrating the discipline to re-engage whenever we find ourselves faltering. The wholeness perspective to running a business does not demand we always live up to the kinds of standards described here, but it does require that we apply everything within our power to do so.

Life will always be filled with choices. I am just grateful to be alive in an era where we no longer have to choose between making money and making a difference. We can now consider a person's spiritual aspirations part of the makeup of a strong, efficient and effective business. Moreover, all of this can be pursued in the best interest of not only the individual (managers and nonmanagers) but also customers, shareholders, providers and the communities where work is performed.

As inspiring as this sounds, most of us are unprepared for all the implications. Incorporating a wide spectrum of spiritual paths into the operational reality of an organization is a relatively new phenomenon, and much needs to be learned about how to engage in such an endeavor in ways that truly optimize business productivity and a person's spiritual integrity. My appeal to you is to participate in this exploration by discussing the possibilities around bridging spirituality and business in your organization and experimenting with perspectives and actions that might further our collective understanding.

4. Companies That Care
Riane Eisler

Riane Eisler is a social scientist, attorney and author best known for her best-seller, *The Chalice and the Blade: Our History, Our Future*, now in 23 foreign editions. Her newest book, *The Real Wealth of Nations: Creating a Caring Economics*, is hailed by Archbishop Desmond Tutu as "a template for the better world we have been so urgently seeking." Her other books include the award-winning *The Power of Partnership* and *Tomorrow's Children: A Blueprint for Partnership Education in the 21st Century*, as well as *Sacred Pleasure*, a daring re-examination of sexuality and spirituality, and *Women, Men and the Global Quality of Life*, documenting the key role of women's status in a nation's general quality of life. She is also the author of more than 300 essays and articles. Dr. Eisler can be contacted at *center@partnershipway.org*. Her personal Web site is *www.rianeeisler.com*.

I — Defining Good Business

The essence of good business is caring. This is not only a spiritual issue or a matter of doing what is right, caring business practices benefit all stakeholders: employees, customers, shareholders and communities.

Caring business policies and practices are actually highly profitable in purely financial terms. The SAS Institute, the world's largest privately held software company, illustrates this point. SAS has the largest on-site daycare operation in North Carolina. Its cafeteria has high chairs and booster seats for children so they can eat with their parents. The company pays the entire cost of health benefits for employees and their domestic partners. Workers are only required to work a seven-hour day, and employees get unlimited sick days, which may be used to care for sick family members. And SAS has had nearly 20 consecutive years of double-digit growth.[1]

What SAS does is to create a work environment that supports employees' well-being on all levels. It leaves them time and energy to have a healthy family life, offers them preventative health and wellness care (as opposed to just sick care), provides education and caregiving for everyone in their families, and helps them with housing. It further offers them stability of employment, an ergonomically safe work environment, and respect for the work they do.

Not surprisingly, applications for jobs at SAS come in by the thousands. Also not surprisingly, SAS workers are committed to making the company successful—and to staying with SAS to enjoy this success. They like the company's more participatory, or "partnership," management style, which encourages communication and is yet another factor in SAS's success.

SAS is one of a growing number of companies that are making more money by giving real value to caring and caregiving. In 2004 the Winning Workplaces' *Fortune Small Business* award went to Carolyn Gable, CEO of New Age Transportation. Gable, a former waitress and single mother of five children, started New Age Transportation out of her home. Thanks to her innovative leadership in creating a tightly knit workplace of intensely loyal workers, it is now a $25 million company. Gable fosters an environment where employees, particularly those with children, can focus on their jobs while still maintaining a healthy work/life balance. She encourages her staff to take care of themselves outside the office by paying for health club memberships and offering employees $250 per quarter for up to a year to quit smoking. And rather than being a drag on profits, these policies led to an average 37 percent yearly growth.[2]

Statistics show that caring business policies sharply reduce employee turnover, saving companies millions of dollars. The cost of replacing hourly employees is equivalent to about six months of their earnings. The cost of replacing salaried employees can be as high as 18 months of their salary. Job turnover can cost as much as 40 percent of annual profits.[3]

Businesses that have more caring policies radically cut turnover and absentee-related losses. Intermedics Inc. decreased its turnover rate by 37 percent with on-site child care, saving 15,000 work hours and $2 million. Virginia Mason Medical Center in Seattle reported 0 percent turnover among employees using its on-site childcare center, compared to about 23 percent turnover among other workers.

Johnson & Johnson found that absenteeism among employees who used flexible work options and family leave policies was an average of 50 percent less than for the workforce as a whole.[4]

Difficulties securing child care are a particularly important factor in the high rates of absenteeism, turnover and, as a consequence, overtime costs in companies with extended-hours operations. A 2003 report by Circadian Technologies Inc. found that extended-hours child care reduces the absenteeism rate by an average of 20 percent. Its study, "Cost Benefits of Child Care for Extended-Hours Operations," found that turnover rates among extended hour employees also decreased substantially when child care services were available—from 9.3 percent to 7.7 percent. Since on average it costs companies $25,000 to recruit and train each new extended-hour employee, this, too, was a big saving.[5]

Caring Private and Public Policies

Of course, these savings don't show the enormous benefits of child-care services to the approximately 28 percent of American women who regularly work nights, evenings or weekends. Nor do they show the benefits to society at a time when latchkey children are a major U.S. concern. As emphasized by Professor Joan C. Williams, director of the Center for WorkLife Law at the University of California Hastings College of the Law, support for caregivers in the formal workforce is not only a business issue but a public policy issue.

〰

Today 37 percent of the workforce has children under age 18. Small wonder that in a Radcliffe survey, 83 percent of women and 82 percent of men aged 21-29 put having time to spend with their families at the top of their priority list, way ahead of a high salary and a prestigious job.[6]

The number of caregivers in the workforce will rise even more dramatically as Americans age. By 2020 the U.S. over-50 population will increase 74 percent compared to 1 percent for those under 50. Polls show that 54 percent of U.S. workers anticipate caring for an elderly parent or relative in the next 10 years.[7]

Reports from the Families and Work Institute and scores of other organizations, as well as books such as Sandra Burud's and Marie Tomolo's *Leveraging the New Human Capital*, show that factoring these realities into workplace policies is not only socially essential; it makes good business sense.[8] A study of clients of the KPMG Emergency Back-up Child-Care program, for example, showed that offering employees childcare yielded a 125 percent return on investment (ROI) within six months and that by the fourth year, the ROI was a whopping 521 percent.[9]

A General Services Administration child care study found that 55 percent of workers who were offered a child-care subsidy were better able to concentrate at work.[10] A study of users of the Bristol Myers Squibb child care centers showed they had a deeper commitment to the company.[11] A Bright Horizons Child Care survey showed that even employees without children feel work-site child care has a positive impact on their workplaces.[12]

In short, caring policies make for happier, more productive workers, stronger families and more fulfilling lives. This leads to higher financial profits, thus, a stronger, more productive economy.

Changing Our Values

Yet many businesspeople still believe the only possibility is a dog-eat-dog, uncaring economics. They think of caring as "soft" or "feminine"—whether it's by a woman or a man— and dismiss it as counterproductive, or at best irrelevant, to business success. The same kind of thinking has distorted national funding priorities.

Many politicians have no problem with huge deficits and large budgets for weapons, wars and prisons. But when it comes to investing in caring for people—health care, child care, paid parental leave and other investments in a better quality of life—they claim there is no money. Of course, the issue is not one of money; it's one of priorities and values.

The Real Wealth of Nations

Ultimately, the real wealth of a nation lies in the quality of its human and natural capital. I should here add that an investment in human capital is an investment in human beings. It is the enhancement of the quality of life of human beings, of human happiness and fulfillment, not just of the ability to earn income in the market. I should also add that by natural capital I don't just mean a nation's natural resources, but also our planet's ecological health. Without this, we risk losing everything, including our lives.

This investment is not only the right and just thing to do; it is essential in purely economic terms as we shift from the industrial to the postindustrial knowledge/information era where "high quality human capital" is the most important capital. Already knowledge and service work represents the vast majority of jobs (85 percent according to business expert Peter Drucker), and even the remaining jobs (15 percent in manufacturing and agriculture) are becoming more knowledge-intensive and interactive.[13]

America and the world are in the midst of a sea change as we shift from the industrial to the knowledge/information era. Many of the jobs being lost in manufacturing and other fields will be gone for good as we move toward more automation and robotics. Economists tell us that the most important capital for the postindustrial economy is "high-quality human capital."

Children are the real wealth of our nation. Investing in a caring society will both stimulate economic recovery and develop the high-capacity human capital capable of pioneering new frontiers of innovation in every sector of society: culturally, socially, technologically and environmentally. It will lead to a more just world and to more fulfilling lives for us all.

Section II

Soulful Leaders

5. Soul Management
Bil and Cher Holton

Rev. Drs. Bil and Cher Holton are licensed Unity ministers serving at Unity Spiritual Life Center in Durham, North Carolina. They are nationally recognized keynote speakers and team-building consultants. Authors of more than 20 business and spiritual books, the Holtons manage to make time for their ballroom dancing and their two sons and three grandchildren. They can be contacted at *www.unityspirituallifecenter.org*.

A convulsing economy characterized by fits and starts is radically altering the workplace—and people's perception of it. The spastic nature of business today is prompting people to question both the essence and motives of business. With their insatiable appetite for downsizing, cutting pensions and health benefits, seeking bankruptcy protection, and short-circuiting people's retirements, many businesses are showing insensitivity and paranoia—symptoms of a loss of soul. Corporate soul does not pour into the bottom line automatically. It requires—no, demands—business leaders who are in touch with their own souls.

The essence of good business, therefore, is *soul management*. You may want to read that sentence again. Soul management is *the* critical success factor in the success of any business. Soul has been defined as "the moral or spiritual part of something." Businesses, like people, have souls whether the leaders who run those businesses believe in a corporate soul or not. Businesses that understand will thrive in shaky economies as well as stable ones.

As businesses strive to understand what good soul management means, they may want to remind themselves of the epicurean principle that holds that the marketplace rewards they are seeking may come from an extraordinarily ordinary place deep within their own organizations, despite their penchant for looking to Wall Street or government bailouts for salvation.

Unfortunately, most of the businesses we have worked with think only in terms of profit and loss, and so the soul elements are left off the ledger. Where there is no consideration of soul, there is a weakening of soul. It seems to us that one of the chief ailments of a majority of businesses today is not so much a lack of efficiency or productivity, but the loss of soul. This soul depletion presents itself, among other things, as defective products and inferior service, disrespect for the environment, faulty metrics, sketchy lending practices and narcissistic executives who line their pockets at the expense of their employees' pensions. As these pathologies suggest, labor without a spiritual base becomes one-dimensional and self-aggrandizing in nature.

It does not have to be that way, of course. Businesses can manage both their secular and spiritual aspects. As a matter of fact, some businesses are modifying their overall perspective about what is important in business and sending their executives and managers to conferences and workshops on spirituality. Many transformational business leaders feel *soiled* by the practice of chasing after profits as their organization's primary corporate value. They are looking for meaningful work and work that is respectful of employees, customers, distributors, suppliers and the environment.

Soul-connected businesses recognize the spiritual leakage that occurs when nature is abused by the polluting of her waterways, air and land with manufacturing waste. They are very much aware that when we compromise the health of our environment in the name of speed and greed, we compromise our own health because our bodies, which are part of the fabric of nature, feel the unhealthy effects. Soul-savvy business leaders know that there is no distinction, no separation, between Mother Nature's body and our own.

Unconscious business leaders, the ones who neglect the soul connection, generally overlook the benefits soulfulness brings to the work setting. Their unwillingness to acknowledge the therapeutics of a soul-conditioned work environment takes the form of plastic plants, fake trees and perfunctory interest in green work environments. Plastic greenery is often an indicator of their plastic commitment.

Good Business

Enlightened business leaders know that all work tasks, procedures and organizational objectives have sacred components, whether they involve entering or collecting data, monitoring business processes, speaking to customers, driving company vehicles, or emptying trash receptacles. Each task, every *molecule of effort*, is important in a soul-managed work environment. And the employees who perform those functions are valued and respected for being in alignment with the sacred dimensions of work.

One-dimensional managers and executives fail to realize that the entire workforce suffers a wound to soul every time shoddy work and compromised quality are condoned. The products of work and the level of service are like a reflection in a pond: an indication of authenticity or an indictment exposing spiritual slippage. Soulless businesses fail to see that worshipping widgets and crunching inflated numbers create rickets in an organization's soul. If shoddy work and idol worship become organizational norms, they will asphyxiate what is left of the corporate soul and leave the business without a spiritual rudder in which to navigate 21st-century marketplace waters.

Although soulful leaders know that market share is the coinage of the business realm, they are also aware that soul management is the treasury. Driven less by the lure of profits and executive pay and more by the moral compass of altruistic work, soul-seasoned leaders and managers build cathedrals of industry that reflect their values and commitment toward eco-spiritual outcomes. These managers have raised their consciousness above the centrifugal force of money and power.

They choose instead to see power and position as sacred contracts and money as a form of energy to be used wisely.

These *soulful* managers create work environments that are not only competitive but embody spiritual values like generosity, reverence, integrity, community, warmth and service. Some companies have installed indoor waterfalls, meditation rooms, labyrinths and prayer chapels. All of theses things charge the work atmosphere with a spiritual tone that sends its energies throughout the entire workplace. Work environments can become principled, nurturing environments that build a sense of community as surely as churches, tabernacles, temples, mosques, ashrams and sweat lodges.

Workplaces can be paths of inner development as much as the spiritual centers we mentioned above. The essence of business, any business, is that it can be a place of spiritual practice. The contributions businesses make, in soul-centered business environments, are contributions for the benefit of others. And it is that soulful outlook that burns away purely egocentric motivations.

Soulless work environments leave people feeling alone, cautious, separated and on guard. Once this feeling pervades the organization's psyche, people repress their spirituality and put on their emotional armor, sensing they are in a hostile work environment. They doubt themselves and do not trust the organization. They may see the company as divisive and myopic in its treatment of employees. This soul-detached orientation leads to restlessness and a pervasive tension which negatively affects the quality of both the work and work relationships.

On the other hand, business leaders who are aware of the sacred dimension of work engineer their work environments to foster a sort of collective inner limitlessness. Employees feel as if the business is a benevolent universe, one that promotes both work and play as well as spiritual growth and professional development. Leaders who shape these environments realize that there is a growing spiritual consciousness filtering through the world that transcends any particular religion or creed. They know that people are awakening to a desire to become more engaged in their work as whole persons—in body, mind and spirit. The leaders themselves are feeling this same soul pull and are responding by retooling their workplaces with spiritual technologies that appeal to the whole person.

We have found that leaders who bring ethics and spiritual values into the workplace enjoy increased productivity and profitability. Employee retention, customer loyalty, brand reputation and commitment to the organization's mission and vision all lead to a healthier and happier company. You may think we are being overly dramatic with this next statement, but we absolutely, positively believe that a more spiritually oriented workplace offers the most enduring competitive advantage in ecologically sensitive and environmentally conscious emerging markets.

Hypersecular business leaders fail to see that in today's highly competitive global markets, most talented people seek out organizations that reflect their inner values, world view and personal ethics. These highly talented people demand employers who provide legitimate opportunities for personal and professional development, quality time off, and community service, not just bigger salaries. Companies that chase the soul out keep highly qualified and talented people away.

There are a growing number of companies that offer employees time and resources in the workplace to hold religious services, study groups and classes. They want to accommodate professionals who are working long hours and juggling ridiculous schedules—employees who don't want to abandon their faith on weekdays.

Two of the biggest indicators of the need for more spirituality in the workplace are frequently overlooked by those who are out of touch with the sacred synergy currently present in most workplaces. First, there are more and more women in the workplace, and women tend to be more spiritually expressive than men. Second, an aging workforce is also a factor. Millions of boomers have outgrown their material pursuits and are looking for spiritual answers to mortality questions.

Those companies that teeter-totter around spirituality miss out on the bottom-line benefits of providing spiritual practices that include quiet rooms for meditation and prayer, centering circles, yoga, breathing exercises, restful contemplative gardens, healing touch, accupressure treatments, spiritual cinemas, lunch-and-learn sessions on spiritual subjects, and classes on how to minimize ecological footprints, to name a few.

There is a definite *feel* when we walk into a business that has depleted or lost its soul. There are staleness and lethargy in the atmosphere—the mental and emotional atmosphere. There is a sense of perpetual triage, a hint of prolonged disconnectedness. On the other hand, there is a vibrancy in those businesses that nurture their soul. We can *feel* the aliveness and positive energy that define this institutionalized spirituality. We can also see peace in the midst of busyness and warmth accompanied by uncompromised professionalism.

We are fans of the possibility that the *sole* management of business will be its *soul* management. A growing number of books, including the one you are reading, reflect a growing national movement to bring spiritual values and ethics into the workplace: *Jesus, CEO, True Work: The Sacred Dimension of Earning a Living, A Life at Work, The Soul of Business, Liberating the Corporate Soul, The Stirring of Soul in the Workplace, What Would the Buddha Do at Work? Spirit at Work, Redefining the Corporate Soul, The Corporate Mystic, Leading With Soul,* and many, many more.

We affirm that all business leaders will soon discover that all work is liturgy. Best practices will become sacraments, honoring employee pensions and health benefits will be considered as tithes to Spirit. The gap between secular business practices and sacred business sacraments will be erased. Businesses will see extraordinary quality and heroic service as new bottom lines. They will use supplies that respect the environment; truly welcome and reward employees' creativity and innovation; and compensate men and women equally. This is our intention. What is yours?

6. The Power of the Seven Cs
John Knowles

John Knowles is the full-time minister/spiritual leader of the
Unity Church of Sheboygan, Wisconsin. He serves on the
Board of Directors of Unity School of Christianity, Unity Village,
Missouri. John incorporated his business, Plymouth Industries,
Inc., in 1986. Located in Plymouth, Wisconsin, it has since
evolved to become a leading custom machinery, design
engineering and manufacturing company. John holds several
patents and has inspired many creative designs that have
served a diverse market. As he turns his business over to
two of his sons to carry forward, John still remains active
as the CEO/chairman of the board.

As long as I can remember, I've had a desire to be a minister; but I ended up being an entrepreneur, an engineer,
a businessman and a father with a great deal of responsibility. All of these responsibilities seemed to take me far, far away
from my dream. Life moved along at a rapid pace and the

desire to minister lay dormant inside my heart, buried so deep that I could barely feel it. In fact, I had completely rationalized that I no longer wanted to be a minister and that it was a misinterpreted desire. After all, I had seven children to help get through college and a business to run. And, everyone knows what a minister earns—it financially seemed impossible.

Then one day I was listening to a taped lecture given by Marianne Williamson. She said, "Within every business is a ministry," and suddenly it clicked. I do not have to wait to become a minister, I have a ministry right where I am. My family is a ministry; my community is a ministry; and imagine that: my business is a ministry. No one is really in the material handling business, or the custom machinery business, or any other type of business. In fact everyone is in the "ministering to people" business; yet so few of us realize the implications or power of this understanding.

The shift in my business was subtle at first, but eventually it started to penetrate the entire organization. It is not as if I had not already understood the necessary component of caring for people, it was just a shift that allowed a more authentic approach that was more consistent and unapologetic. More of the traditional business approaches dropped away, excuses like "It isn't good business," "We will set a bad precedent," "We can't do that—it isn't written in the employee manual," "How can that be financially responsible?" "Why should we care? It isn't our problem," "Isn't that being codependent?" "It is none of our business," "We will get into legal trouble," and every other excuse not to help, not to get involved or not to show true compassion to our employees. Somehow this shift in thinking—the discovery that we were in the people business—helped me look at circumstance in new ways, and that made all the difference.

Zig Ziglar said, "People don't care how much you know until they know how much you care." Caring can never be a strategy, it must be real and from the heart because people can detect a phony a mile and a half away. If you do not feel it, don't do it, because you are wasting your time and theirs. However, if behind your action is an intention to care more, be more, be a part of a higher possibility for all concerned, then even if you don't pull it off the first few times, keep perfecting the art because it offers huge rewards. It is really a heartfelt art to care for people, because there are no rules. All that is needed is a sincere desire to help, a sincere desire to serve, a sincere desire to heal, to be part of the solution, to be a light unto the world, and make things better than you found them.

Business leaders need to embody this new model of leadership, the enlightened leader. Personally, it calls to my creative side, as every situation is different, every individual's needs are different, and, therefore, every application of our caring must be administered uniquely. If we do it from a "you're broken and I'm going to fix you" approach, we are probably coming from ego. If we are coming from "you are my subordinate and I am here to help you," we are probably coming from ego. If we are coming from "this is good for my business, therefore, I must do the right thing," we are probably coming from ego. True compassion wells up from inside us, and our ego-needs are relegated to a minor role. Our only goal is to help, heal, lead, teach, love and know the Truth within the situation so we can be a light unto the world.

The universe loves harmony. We all love harmony. Everyone wants to work in a situation where they are an important part of a well-tuned system, where people around them care beyond "what have you done for me lately." The truth is money loves harmony as well and is attracted to great harmonious purpose. The true measure of our bottom line is really an outward expression of how well we have applied solid, enlightened management principles in our lives and our businesses.

Here are some general guidelines that will help you evaluate whether you are an enlightened leader who really understands the significance of the meaning that there is a ministry within every business. If you think it is important to treat all people equally, this will not work. The enlightened model only requires that you treat people fairly and compassionately. How in the world could you treat all totally unique individuals the same? It takes unique action to deal with unique individuals!

If you think that you cannot be demanding and that you are there to put up with unacceptable behavior, you are missing the point. An enlightened leader understands that even one bad apple spoils the rest and unproductive behavior has to be dealt with in creative and compassionate ways. Most undesirable or deviant behavior usually has nothing to do with what is seen and everything to do with what is not seen. Until you understand what is really going on, you are only going to make matters worse. Enlightened leaders always remember that people need understanding and compassion the most when they deserve it the least. Grace from the leader, when properly given, brings in huge rewards and huge loyalty ... again, when properly administered.

Personal relationships with employees will give some people the idea that they are special and that they get special privileges. The enlightened leader makes everyone special and everyone gets special privileges, but only when they really need them. The enlightened leader must always consider the specific and special needs of the individuals and the requirements of the company. The needs of the whole must be strongly considered. The purpose of the organization is to survive. Without the organization, none of the needs of any of the employees or customers can be served. At times the survival of the organization must be put first, and when that is properly communicated, everyone will be in agreement.

Every organization is only as healthy as the workforce. Exceptional productivity is possible only if the employees are healthy. Most businesses invest a lot of time maintaining their equipment, but invest little or no resources in maintaining their people. On the other hand, employees respect a company that cares and promotes good health. This is really part of a successful safety and productivity program. People feel good about themselves when they are healthy and productive. Enlightened leadership encourages health and sets high standards for productivity, safety and quality. These standards become the culture of the workplace. People go home tired, but very satisfied ... very happy that they were vital contributors.

Only after many years of consistent effort will employees start believing and trusting the reliability of management information; the assurance of fair, timely and appropriate decisions; and the company's good-faith effort to do the right thing in every situation. Communication is paramount, and effective listening is absolutely required. The egoist boss style of issuing dictatorial directives is so far from effective that it is a wonder why supervisors ever thought it was an option. Remember it is not what you say; it is not just what you do; it is the vibration from which it came!

After a while people are so used to being treated like people, like valued partners, like someone who matters, like an associate, like a vital part of something bigger than themselves, they could never imagine working for a company that was not similar. The decrease in stress increases creativity, and the harmony and joy of doing something right brings pride that perpetuates itself and permeates the entire company from the sweeper to the president. The hierarchy is largely unnoticed and the power struggles largely disappear for a larger agenda. This does not mean there is no conflict; it just means the conflict has been managed in a positive and constructive way that fully honors everyone.

There are no special rules to determine just how enlightened leadership is modeled; however, when you walk through a company that has it, you can feel it immediately. It is part of the walls, part of the machinery, and part of every employee. When people tour our plant, some of them are enlightened enough to feel that intangible compassion that is at the heart of our company and they try to tell me what they feel. They say, "Wow! Everyone seems to get along so well and they are so productive. Everything is so organized and clean. You sure have a great company here!" Rarely do they know, except perhaps on a subconscious level, what they are feeling. What they feel is the compassion that has been part of our culture for many years.

The intangible heart shown by enlightened leaders manifests in tangible ways as well, like in your absentee record. It shows up in the safety record. A poor safety record, a high turnover rate, poor quality issues, and legal problems can be leading indicators that a company is not being led by an enlightened leader. If you are not making it financially, chances are the leadership has not created an atmosphere of harmony, trust and balance. Again, money loves harmony but evaporates in chaos, mistrust and egoistic environments and in situations that have not been consistently handled in accordance with the high standards of a creative, enlightened culture.

A great business is built on great decisions. In most businesses there are three or four important decisions that must be handled properly every year, any of which improperly handled could put the company in danger of extinction. Naturally, it is important to make these big decisions carefully, but I believe an enlightened business also handles the small decisions well. For it is the $50 decisions made poorly, thousands of times over, that slowly drain the life force of the business. The true cost is much higher than it appears because poorly made decisions have a very demoralizing impact on everybody in the workforce. So much buy-in is lost. So much opportunity to capitalize on momentum that never happens. So much lost energy.

Enlightened leadership is a way of life. It is an art form that is developed through the wise application of true caring and the creative application of simple, practical, principles: unconditional caring, compassion, kindness, the desire to do the right things, the understanding of the law of giving and receiving, and the connection within yourself that puts you in alignment with a higher purpose and Power. You become, as Thoreau said, "a higher order of being," or in other words, an enlightened leader. Companies that are led by enlightened leaders are, in my experience, rare indeed; but the world of business is shifting more in that direction every day. Changing times require new leaders; leaders who can run companies in enlightened ways for an awakening world.

Our planet has seven seas. Enlightened business also have seven Cs:

1. **Communication:** Caring has to be communicated in every decision, every time, everywhere ... over and over and over again.

2. **Creativity:** People are all unique. To try to treat them all equally or all the same just does not work. Unique people require unique and creative approaches that always look different but always have the highest and best for all concerned as the main theme. In a corporate culture where people are treated with fairness and compassion,

they become far more creative. Creative, effective problem-solving becomes a natural part of the culture.

3. **Consult:** Management doesn't have all the answers. To ask or involve people in the decision-making process always yields an improved decision and creates great employee buy-in. Consult your inner knowing; if it does not feel right, it probably isn't!

4. **Compassion:** Compassion, unconditional caring, kindness and true concern are not strategies. Only true heartfelt actions yields lasting results. Remember showing true concern must often be extended when it seems like it is deserved the least.

5. **Competitive advantage:** Your workforce is one of your main competitive advantages. When you have a workforce that has been treated with respect and fairness for years and years, they will have learned to trust you to always do the right thing, and great loyalty and productivity become the norm.

6. **Comparison:** Honor diversity. No two people are the same. No two organizations are the same. No two applications of enlightened action are the same. Only through wise listening to what is actually happening can the correct action be administered.

7. **Culture:** A long-range result of the consistent, compassionate application of caring and concern is a safer, more productive, less stressed-out workforce. These workers are loyal beyond compare because they have experienced compassionate leaders who care about

their personal concerns. This creates a culture where people feel they are protected by their leaders—enlightened leaders who truly care. Remember, all businesses are ministries in disguise!

7. The Path of Leadership Progress
Stephen Blumberg

Stephen K. (Steve) Blumberg, Ph.D., is a professor emeritus at California State University, Long Beach, in the Master of Public Administration (M.P.A.) degree program. Dr. Blumberg received the University's Distinguished Faculty Teaching Award and was twice named the College of Health and Human Services' Most Valuable Professor. He is a former two-term mayor of Manhattan Beach, California, and was the Director of Community Relations for Chicago's Leadership Council for Metropolitan Open Communities, an agency established as a result of Dr. Martin Luther King Jr.'s 1966 Chicago marches.

Would you like to work in a place where people look forward to coming to work every day? Of course you would! "But," you say, "that's just silly! People go to work because they have to make a living—they have to pay the bills." Unfortunately, too often this is true; too often people put up with generally unpleasant work situations because they feel they have to.

Well, it does not have to be this way! It is absolutely possible to create work environments where positive, spiritual principles such as those taught by Unity serve as the underlying foundation for an organization's atmosphere. These positive, spiritual principles include compassion, tolerance, honesty, kindness and appreciation. Indeed, these principles can be summarized by the Golden Rule. It is truly more than a cliché to "do unto others as you would have them do unto you."

This notion of treating others the way we would like to be treated applies to people throughout the workplace. Being kind to your co-workers; demonstrating concern for your colleagues; respecting the feelings of the people you interact with are attitudes and behaviors that can easily be practiced by all of us irrespective of our position in the organization. In other words, it matters not whether you are part of the clerical support staff, a supervisor, a sales associate, a vice president or one of the custodians. All you need to do is go through your day at work showing that *you care about people.*

The essential focus of this essay is *good business,* and there must be no misunderstanding in terms of what is absolutely critical for there to be good business in any organization. The critical factor is *productivity,* results, the achievement of goals, the bottom line.

And good business and productivity are inextricably related to caring about people. While it is clear that everybody throughout an organization can help to create an atmosphere of caring and concern, it is management that has ultimate responsibility. Management sets the tone and provides an example. What follows, then, is a blueprint or road map for effective leadership. This road map is a concept created during my early years as a university professor, called the "Organizational Path of Progress." The concept of a "path of progress" recognizes that there is an intense interrelationship among the various elements in an organization and that these elements can be woven together to achieve good business. This map uses the metaphor of a path. It is important to remember that progress along a path happens one step at a time. Obviously, if there is a blockage at any point along the path, progress is halted.

The Organizational Path of Progress begins with the *leadership* of the organization. She may be the minister or spiritual vice president; he may be the chairman or manager. It is not the title with which we are concerned; it is the position, and those who are blessed with positions of leadership must understand that even if they don't realize it, they are playing a vital role in establishing the climate that is pervasive throughout their organization.

To begin a path of progress, we need capable leaders who know themselves well enough to lead with confidence. A self-confident leader is secure about his or her own ability and knowledge. Feeling secure prevents leaders from feeling threatened by bright people in their organization. Self-confident leaders have *confidence in themselves and in the people they are managing*.

Managerial confidence in people throughout the organization leads to the next step along the path of progress. This step is *open communication*. This involves sharing information, enabling everyone to feel aware of what is going on. Knowing what's going on can lead to people being more willing to share their workplace problems and concerns. This leads to the next step on our path: people feeling as though they have a *common stake* in their organization.

People feeling that they have a common stake, fostered by open communication, leads to *participation*. Good leaders encourage and promote the participation of others, and others welcome these opportunities to participate. This participation leads to constructive *involvement* in the organization's activities, and involvement stimulates enduring *commitment*.

Before continuing our journey along the path of progress, let us pause to ponder an equation that encapsulates these last few steps along the path. The formula is $P + I = C$. Participation and involvement lead to commitment. We can state as a truism: People who have opportunities to be involved with what is going on in their workplace are more willing to do what needs to be done to achieve results.

As organizational members experience participation, involvement and commitment, they begin to feel as though they are a valued member of the team. This promotes the next step on the path: a *sense of purpose*. This sense of purpose provides employees a meaningful reason for coming to work. Having an organization full of people who want to come to work, who feel a sense of purpose, will certainly maximize *organizational effectiveness*, which is the seventh step along the path of progress. Effectiveness is measured by productivity—the results we achieve from committed people **wanting** to accomplish tasks rather than being forced, coerced or ordered to do so.

Productive individuals reach the eighth step on the path—job *satisfaction*. The achievement of job satisfaction moves us on to the ninth step—*contentment*. Contentment promotes feelings of *self-actualization*, the 10th step. Self-actualization can be defined as a sense that "I am working toward realizing my full potential." Participating, being a member of a team that achieves good results, and fully using our talents and abilities allow our sense of self-actualization to flourish.

These first 10 steps along the path of progress foster an organizational spirit of *cooperative teamwork*, step 11. Teamwork leads to the 12th step of the path—*organizational humanism*. It matters not whether we use terminology such as *organizational democracy, participatory management* or any other term. What must be understood is that moving through this path of progress enables leaders to create *humane organizations*.

The ultimate beneficiary of humane organizations is the broader society. Thus, the final step is the *societal benefit* resulting from the completion of the path of progress. Indeed, a wonderful wealth of benefits result from the productive, creative, self-actualized members of a society who emerge from humane organizations. After all, employees are also a part of the broader society. Their lives certainly are, among other things, shaped and influenced by what they experience at work. There can be little doubt that their work experience has a profound impact on how these folks will then relate to society. Persons who are fortunate to work in "good business" organizations that have followed this path of progress will have a more positive impact on society. It is only natural that people leaving these humane organizations at the end of their workday will then be more apt to transmit these same positive feelings to those with whom they interact outside their organizations. In other words, the existence of a more satisfied, fulfilled workforce leads directly to a more productive, fulfilled society.

Our society needs good businesses where leaders have a sincere concern for people. Those of us in positions of organizational leadership know that our responsibility is awesome, and we accept that responsibility. We understand that policies focusing on productivity without an honest concern for those who are expected to achieve this productivity are policies that stand self-condemned. Creating humane workplaces is a prerequisite to achieving a just society.

8. Executive Evocateurs

John P. Schuster

John P. Schuster is an author, speaker and mentor to execu-
tives. His books include: *The Power of Open-Book
Management* (Wiley & Sons, 1996), translated into four lan-
guages; *The Open-Book Management Field Book* (1998);
Hum-Drum to Hot-Diggity on Leadership (2001); *and
Answering Your Call: A Guide to Living Your Deepest Purpose*
(Berrett Koehler, 2003), translated into Spanish and French. For
more information, contact *www.johnpschuster.com.*

As leaders move higher in an organization, they gain
increased authority, but the power to execute their
plans is increasingly in the hands of the doers: middle managers down to the front-line performers. In other words, as
authority increases, the power to execute decreases. This can
be a problem, but the best leaders know how to succeed by
mastering "second-hand power."

Second-Hand Power to Execute

Second-hand power is "the power to evoke." The executives who are good at this skill set are *executive evocateurs.*
Executive-evoking power begins with the kind and quality of
feedback provided. Everything an executive or a manager
says is important in the eyes of others in the organization (at
least until they blow their credibility). Executives often forget
what power they have projected upon them by their follow-
ers. Lower-level managers compete, grovel and can even
make themselves sick over the desire for a word of praise or
encouragement from the senior vice president or the president. It takes clear intention and lots of heart to harness this
power for its most useful purpose; that is, evoking great
things out of the people who execute the work.

When this part of executive work is done well, the leader
will be remembered for the rest of his or her life. I know this
from conversations with top executives and managers about
the people who made a difference in their lives or careers.
Although some of the examples are recent, many of those I
hear about go back years, even decades. They recount stories
about how the latent talent within them was tapped by their
boss; *how they turned a corner on who they thought they were and
what they thought they were able to accomplish.* And they tell you
like it was yesterday, their memories are so vivid.

Calling forth potential—being an evocateur—is a talent.
The managers and executives who do it have the desire to do
it. They know they are delving deeply into a person's heart
and soul to find the untouched promise the individual holds.
Let's look at how they do it.

Executive Evocateurs at Work

There are several ways that executive evocateurs have an impact on the people within their organizations, building their capability to execute:

Executive evocateurs accept others as they are, not as people who are flawed or wanting. They understand that an unpolished gemstone of a potential leader will become brighter only with polish. They understand that the key to knowing who and when to polish is first accepting the person, blemishes and all, just as she/he is. Then and only then can the executive evocateur move into polishing.

Executive evocateurs see what others see, but they think something different. In viewing an emerging leader, executive evocateurs see what is, as well as what can be. At a prominent medical device company in Minnesota, a woman was hired as a temp and placed in the Clinical Affairs department, processing the data that resulted from the use of new devices being tested for FDA approval. Look ahead 10 years, and she is a clinical research manager, with many people reporting to her. She has lived through a company acquisition and numerous organizational restructurings. She has traveled for business frequently and has earned the acknowledgement and respect of company leaders. Her potential for this kind of responsibility was spotted; and she was taught, groomed and promoted—all because someone saw her potential.

Executive evocateurs appeal to the innate human longing to be more than we are. They neither dismiss others' aspirations nor step on their dreams. They know not to accept who they are seeing in front of their eyes at face value. They are not like one nonevocateur, who told a young secretary who had decided to return to college, "You'll never make it." Not only did he not appeal to her longing to develop herself, he cynically commented on her chances. But his remark did not discourage her. She did indeed "make it," completing a B.A. after many years of working, attending school and raising a child. But those words, and the smug expression on the face of the "leader" who said them, were never forgotten.

Executive evocateurs both find and create teachable moments. They have the talent of discernment, of knowing if the right time has come or making the time right as opportunities present themselves. They take advantage of an employee's capability to soak up the lessons that are available to him or her. If they act too early or too late, the window is gone.

Executive evocateurs adapt their methods. They have developed more than one way to listen, to challenge, to provide feedback and to acknowledge. They work with what they're working with. And they know when to push hard and when value will be lost by doing so. One student said of her accomplished teacher, the famous Dorothy Delay of the Juilliard School of Music: "Her method is that she has no method. She figures out how the student thinks and goes there."

Executive evocateurs work at the level of identity. When you have had a real evocateur for your boss, you know you will never be the same. Something deep changes and it changes permanently. One explanation for this is that the evocateur changes not just the way you think; he or she challenges and sharpens your values. The person who once was interested in customers becomes passionate about customers. The person who wanted to build an adequate team now wants to create the highest-performing team possible. The person who wanted a good career *now* wants to make a difference.

Executive evocateurs acknowledge. They are not holdovers from the old belief that an occasional pat on the head and "attaboy" is sufficient. They know that the need for acknowledgement for real contribution is one of the deepest motivators in human life. They know that a word of praise when it is sincere could well be remembered for a lifetime.

How do you know if you have done any of the above; that is, if you have been an executive evocateur? There is a simple measure. You hear people say things like this about you and your organization: "I was proud to be a part of the organization, and on your team. I was at my best when I was there." That is the kind of reaction that makes leadership worthwhile. Are you up to the task?

9. Reconstructing Our Idea of Leadership

Peter Block

Peter Block is the author of several best-selling books: *Flawless Consulting: A Guide to Getting Your Expertise Used* (1980); *The Empowered Manager: Positive Political Skills at Work* (1987); and *Stewardship: Choosing Service Over Self-Interest* (1993). His latest book is *Community: The Structure of Belonging* (Berrett Koehler, 2008). He has also authored *The Answer to How Is Yes: Acting on What Matters*, which won the 2002 Independent Publisher Book Award for Business Breakthrough Book of the Year. He co-authored *Freedom and Accountability at Work: Applying Philosophic Insight to the Real World* with consultant and philosopher Peter Koestenbaum (Jossey-Bass/Pfeiffer, 2001). Peter Block is the recipient of the Organization Development Network's 2008 Lifetime Achievement Award. In 2004 he received their first place Members' Choice Award, which recognized *Flawless Consulting* as the most influential book for OD practitioners over the past 40 years. Visit Peter's Web sites at *www.peterblock.com*, *www.designedlearning.com* and *www.asmallgroup.net* or contact him at *pbi@att.net.*

Leadership is the capacity to initiate a future distinct from the past. This is what distinguishes leadership from management. Management is the capacity to give order and structure in service of high performance. Management is not burdened with an act of creation, it is about operationalizing goals and objectives.

A distinct future can be achieved only through high engagement. We can say then that the essence of leadership is about convening, valuing relatedness, and decentralizing its own role. It is not a personality characteristic or a matter of style and, therefore, it requires nothing more than what all of us already have. In this way, "leader" belongs right up there with cook, carpenter, artist and landscape designer. It is a capacity that can be learned by all of us, with a small amount of teaching, and an agreement to practice—the ultimate do-it-yourself project.

An alternative future, sometimes called *transformation*, occurs when a community of people chooses to come together and be accountable for something larger than itself. All we know about learning, exceptional performance and creativity indicates that the existence of a supportive community is what makes the difference. Leadership in these terms becomes community building.

What community building requires is a concept of the leader as one who creates experiences for others—experiences that, in themselves, are an example of, or in support of, a desired future. For example, if we seek a culture of agility, customer focus, learning and commitment, then these qualities need to be present every time we come together. The experiences we create need to be designed in such a way that agility, care for the wants of others, openness to surprise and commitment are experienced and demonstrated.

Engagement Is the Point

Engagement is at the heart of this new way of thinking about leadership. This is very different from the conventional belief that the task of leadership is to set a vision, enroll others in it, and hold people accountable through measurements and reward. Most current leadership writings and trainings reinforce these conventional beliefs that:

- Leaders are essential. They are role models who need to possess a special set of personal skills.

- The task of the leader is to define the destination and create the blueprint to get there.

- The leader's work is to bring others on board. Enroll, align, inspire.

- Leaders provide (and define) the oversight, measurement and training needed of others.

Each of these beliefs elevates leaders as an elite group, singularly worthy of special development, coaching and incentives. All of these beliefs have face validity; however they also have unintended consequences such as isolation, entitlement and passivity—consequences that our organizations and communities cannot afford.

The Art of Convening

The paradigm shift is to believe that the task of leadership is to provide context and produce engagement—to tend to our social fabric. In this way, new paradigm leadership has three tasks:

1. Create a context that nurtures an alternative future, one based on gifts, generosity, accountability and commitment.

2. Initiate and convene conversations that shift people's experience. This occurs as a result of the way people are brought together and the nature of the questions used to engage them.

3. Listen, pay attention and refrain from giving answers and advice.

Convening leaders put people in small groups and use questions to create the social space within which members/employees/citizens become deeply engaged. Through this engagement, they discover that it is in their power to resolve something or at least move the action forward. This is what triggers the choice to be accountable for those things over which they can have power, even though they may have no control.

Listening as an Action

In addition to convening a meeting and naming the question, listening is a critical role of leadership. Listening may be the single most powerful action the leader can take. Leaders will always be under pressure to speak, but if building social fabric is important and sustained transformation is the goal, then listening becomes the greater service.

The Convening Role of Elected Officials

Elected officials are a special case of how we think about leadership and the art of convening. We have put elected officials in a difficult role. We distort them into service providers and suppliers. We relate to them as if we are consumers, not citizens. We want them to solve for us those issues that we should be solving for ourselves.

The customer model, where elected officials exist to satisfy citizen demands, is a disservice to community, even though citizens love it. Elected officials are partners with citizens, not suppliers. The most useful role that elected officials can perform is to bring citizens together. They have a convening capacity unlike anyone else, but it is greatly underutilized.

For Example: Cold Spring

Mark Stoeber is the mayor of Cold Spring, Kentucky, a small and mostly residential town. At some point he realized that the citizen complaints he was hearing did not need an elected official to resolve. For example, he was getting complaints in one neighborhood about someone's dog. Mark decided that the complaint about the dog was a symptom of the lack of connectedness among neighbors.

With the dog's behavior as a cover, he asked one citizen to host a meeting in his home with other neighbors. Neighbors showed up, including the dog owner, and some agreement was reached. Social fabric became a little stronger. Dogs were better behaved. The mayor moved on to more important things.

A year later, Mark decided to take another step and invited about 20 community leaders into a conversation with city council members. They met in council chambers, but not in the usual configuration. In Cold Spring, as in most cities, the council sits on a platform and citizens sit on a lower level. For this meeting, everyone sat in chairs in circles in the council room. They arranged themselves in groups to sit with people they knew the least and talked about some of the city's critical questions: the crossroads at which the city found itself; the major gifts of the city and its citizens; their doubts about anything really changing; a look at the future demands facing the city; and ways more people might be engaged in this conversation. This was a small but symbolic beginning for an elected official who decided that the future economic development and quality of life for the city was dependent on the quality of relatedness of its citizens and their ability to bring those on the margin into the center.

You can easily see how these examples are relevant to businesses. Instead of investing so much in training people and infusing them with new skills, we would be better off helping employees discover their own capacity to own and create the future. Bosses, if they saw themselves as conveners, would view their employees as a community waiting to be engaged.

To summarize: None of this is an argument against leaders or leadership, only a desire to change the nature of how we think about their responsibilities. Creating a new future hinges on widespread accountability and connectedness. This requires leaders who convene people in new ways to create conditions where context and focus shift:

- From a place of fear and fault to one of gifts, generosity and abundance.

- From a bet on measurement and oversight to one of social fabric and voluntary accountability.

- From a focus on leader advice to a focus on evoking the wisdom, capacities and ownership of citizens.

When we train leaders, we should get off the vision and style wagon and help them learn about convening, questioning and listening. This allows us to de-glamorize egocentric leadership and redefine leadership as the capacity to create transformational communities. Our future depends on it!

10. The New Leadership Agenda
Richard Barrett

Richard Barrett is the founder and chairman of the Barrett
Values Centre. He is an internationally recognized consultant
and keynote speaker on values-based leadership. Barrett is the
author of *A Guide to Liberating Your Soul* (1995), *Liberating the
Corporate Soul: Building a Visionary Organization* (1998), and
*Building a Values-Driven Organization: A Whole System
Approach to Cultural Transformation* (2006). He is a contributing author to *Psychometrics in Coaching (2008)* (Chapter 15:
"Coaching for Cultural Transformation"). Richard is a Fellow of
the World Business Academy and former Values Coordinator at
the World Bank. He is the creator of the internationally recognized Cultural Transformation Tools, which have been used to
support more than 1,000 organizations in 42 countries in
their transformational journeys. For more information, visit
www.valuescentre.com or e-mail *Richard@valuescentre.com.*

Good Business

༺

Never before in history has the leadership of human affairs been more critical than it is now. The decisions made in the next two decades will determine the future of humanity. The well-being of billions of people and the viability of our planet's life-support systems are at stake. The situation is more complex than ever before because the crises we are facing are global, but the systems of governance we have for dealing with them are primarily national.

The difficulties we are experiencing stem from two sources: a) an exaggerated belief in the concept of national sovereignty (the self-interest of nations) and b) global institutions that are dominated and compromised by the self-interest of the most powerful nations.

Even though many governments and international institutions recognize the interdependence and interconnectedness of our financial and life-support systems, our politicians are so wrapped up in the self-interest of their nations, the communities that they represent, and the companies and interest groups that fund their re-election campaigns, that they are unable to implement policies which would benefit the global common good. In addition, the most powerful nations are continually manipulating our global institutions to their own political ends.

At the same time, our global corporations, some of which are economically more powerful than the majority of nations, are also pursuing their own self-interests in search of greater financial returns for their owners or investors. For them the environment and ecosystems are regarded as externalities and the well-being of the masses is of little concern.

༺

Investment strategies follow the path of least cost and least resistance, which almost always results in sacrificing the good of the whole for the self-interest of the few.

It is time to recognize that policies and strategies that promote self-interest will not solve the problems of existence we are now facing. We need our political and business leaders to set aside their narrow self-interests and embrace a collaborative approach that supports the well-being of humanity and the planet as a whole.

Political leaders must give up their parochial self-interest and their exaggerated, false belief in national sovereignty. Business leaders must recognize that business is a wholly-owned subsidiary of society and the planet, and they must stop seeking to be the best *in* the world and start seeking to be the best *for* the world. If we lose our environment and life-support systems, we will lose our economy. If the pain of the masses reaches critical proportions, particularly in the rich nations, then the greed and self-interest of our financial and business leaders will no longer be tolerated.

What is being called forth is a global paradigm shift—a shift from a world focused on self-interest to a world focused on the common good. In the future, we will only succeed individually if everyone in our global society succeeds. We simply cannot solve our problems with the same level of thinking that created them.

The following statement by Willis Harman, co-founder of the World Business Academy, rings more true each year.

Business has become the most powerful institution on the planet. The dominant institution in any society needs to take responsibility for the whole. But business has not had such a tradition. This is a new role, not well understood or accepted. So business has to adopt a tradition it has never had throughout the entire history of capitalism: to share responsibility for the whole. Every decision that is made, every action that is taken, must be viewed in the light of that responsibility.[1]

So what are the implications of this situation for business leaders? Who are the new business leaders? What qualities do they need to possess? What is the new leadership agenda?

Resilience

First and foremost, business leaders need to know how to build resilient organizational cultures. To do this they will need to recognize that organizations are living entities. They are human group structures that operate like complex, adaptive systems, just like all other living entities. Living entities are able to survive and thrive only because each individual entity in a group structure has learned that its self-interest is wrapped up in supporting the good of the whole. So the question then becomes, How do leaders create cultures that behave like living entities?

We only have to examine a cell or the human body to find the answer. A cell survives and thrives when the atoms that make up the cell have first learned how to become viable and independent in their frameworks of existence. They next have to learn how to bond with other viable independent atoms to create group structures called molecules, which in turn have to learn how to cooperate with each other to form a higher-order entity: the cell.

We could equally say that human beings are able to survive and thrive because the cells that make up the body learned at some point in the past how to become viable and independent in their frameworks of existence, then learned how to bond with each other to form group structures called organs, which in turn learned how to cooperate with each other to form a higher-order entity, the human body. Each cell in the human body has a job. Each cell knows what to do and can be trusted to work for the good of the whole. This works fine until one cell decides to pursue its own self-interest. We call this cancer. The cancer cell, because it knows no bounds to its self-interest, eventually threatens the good of the whole. It basically stops working for the common good.

Organizations survive and thrive when employees learn how to become viable and independent in their frameworks of existence; then learn how to bond to form teams or business units, and the business units learn how to cooperate with each other to form a higher-order entity called the organization. Self-interest on the part of employees, managers or executives creates cancerous conditions, which, left unchecked, sap the energy of the organization and its ability to survive.

The idea that strong bonds and internal cooperation build successful human group structures is not new. The 14th-century thinker Ibn Khaldun noticed that the most successful tribes in North Africa operated with *asabiya*, which can be translated as "a capacity for collective action."[2] In order for groups not to fall apart, the level of asabiya had to be strongest at the highest level of leadership. To be successful, the decision-making entity of a group (leadership team) must operate as one. We can also translate asabiya as "alignment, social capital or working for the common good." The glue that creates a capacity for collective action is trust.

Basically, organizations work best when all employees are accountable for their specific contributions to the team or business unit; when all business units cooperate rather than compete; and when all employees, managers and executives share the same values and the same sense of purpose.

Our research at the Barrett Values Centre supports this hypothesis. We have found, based on over 1,000 values assessments of organizations in more than 50 countries, that the most resilient organizations have strong values alignment and low levels of cultural entropy—the degree of dysfunction in a system caused by behaviors that are rooted in self-interest.[3]

Adaptability

Second, business leaders need to know how to build adaptable organizations. In *Strategy at the Edge of Chaos*, Beinhocker describes the modern economy as a complex adaptive system. He states, "Markets exhibit periods of relative calm and stability which are interrupted by stormy periods. Such disequilibriums make it difficult for participants to survive for long periods as their strategies, skills or culture tends to get finely optimized for stable periods, and then suddenly becomes obsolete when the restructuring occurs."[4]

Beinhocker goes on to state that "companies have a hard time surviving upheavals, market shakeouts and technology shifts. Therefore, strong cultures are only valuable if they exhibit adaptive and learning qualities. Otherwise, they become a liability during the periods of accelerated change."[5]

I strongly believe that the recent economic meltdown is not a market shakeout or a technology shift. It is the breakdown of an unsustainable economic paradigm that threatens the global sustainability of our human society.

The failure of our financial system, together with global climate change, global terrorism and the increased risk of global pandemics is not only severely testing the resilience and adaptability of our businesses, it is also testing the resilience and adaptability of our global society. Our business and political leaders need to learn how to build strong adaptive cultures.

In a four-year study of 200 organizations, Kotter and Heskett of the Harvard Business School found that companies with strong adaptive cultures outperformed companies with rigid or weak cultures by significant margins. Revenues grew four times faster, the rate of job creation was seven times higher, and stock price grew 12 times faster. Adaptable cultures minimize their cultural entropy by reducing bureaucracy, hierarchy, status, internal competition and blame. In other words, they minimize the impact of self-interest.[6]

The Societal Imperative

Third, business leaders need to understand that in the rapidly approaching new world paradigm, behaviors that in any way compromise the good of our global society will no longer be tolerated. Business is becoming a wholly-owned subsidiary of society, both figuratively and literally—75 percent of the banking system in the United Kingdom is now "owned" by the government. This means in the future businesses will need to share responsibility for the whole not only by supporting our political leaders in defining a framework of policies that support our global society, but also by developing industry charters that regulate the rules of competition between companies in specific sectors in a manner that supports the global policy framework. It behooves every industry to build its own industry charter so that it aligns with this global framework of policies. A good starting point for the development of an industry charter is the Earth Charter (see *www.earthcharterinaction.org*).

Going back to our metaphor of an organization as a living entity, what we are talking about here are viable independent group structures (companies) cooperating to support the evolution of a higher-order entity (our global society).

The New Leader

If we are to survive and thrive in this new world, we will need to develop a new leadership paradigm. Our new leaders will need to be developed, trained and coached in the qualities and attributes that represent the three stages of evolution. Each stage represents a progressively higher level of consciousness:

1. Personal mastery—becoming viable and independent in your framework of existence.

2. Internal cohesion—bonding together with other viable independent entities to form group structures.

3. External cohesion—cooperating with other group structures to create a higher order entity that operates for the good of the whole.

Personal mastery: Our new leaders need to be self-actualized individuals who have successfully learned how to tame the fear-based beliefs which keep them operating out of self-interest and prevent them from operating on behalf of the common good. In other words, they must have learned how to become viable independent beings—viable, in that they are masters of the skills necessary to operate with low personal entropy, and independent, in that they are true to themselves and operate in an authentic manner. The preconditions for personal mastery are the abilities to:

1. Transcend personal conditioning.
2. Transcend cultural conditioning.
3. Become responsible and accountable for one's life.
4. Develop emotional intelligence skills.

Internal cohesion: The new leaders need to be skilled in supporting others in becoming viable independent human beings and inspiring them to bond together to form group structures. They need to be clear about their own sense of mission or purpose and live out this purpose with passion. The preconditions for internal cohesion are the abilities to:

1. Focus on their own personal growth and self-knowledge.
2. Find a personal sense of meaning.
3. Develop their social intelligence skills.
4. Embrace values-based decision-making.

External cohesion: The new leaders need to be able to build alliances and coalitions with other like-minded groups so they can collaborate with each other to create a higher-order entity that operates for the good of the whole and the good of our global society.

The preconditions for external cohesion are the abilities to:

1. Deepen personal growth by developing empathy, humility and compassion.

2. Actualize sense of purpose by making a difference.

3. Become a coach and mentor to members of their group structure.

4. Embrace intuition-based decision-making.

Conclusion

Ultimately, the problems we now face are issues of consciousness, and the crisis we face is a crisis of leadership. We will only get beyond this stage of our collective evolution if we can put aside our narrow self-interests, focus on the whole system, and build a values-driven framework of policies that support the common good. Our business leaders need to step up to this challenge. Business needs to be seen as part of the solution, not part of the problem. Business needs to set an example: to identify, develop and promote leaders who fit the new leadership paradigm.

11. The Leader as Spiritual Agent
Margaret Wheatley

Margaret Wheatley is an internationally acclaimed speaker and writer and president emerita of the Berkana Institute (*www.berkana.org*). Meg's path-breaking book, *Leadership and the New Science*, was first published in 1992 and has been translated into more than 20 languages. It is a standard text in many leadership programs and has won notable awards, including "Best Management Book of 1992" in *Industry Week*, "Top Ten Business Books of the 1990s" in *CIO Magazine* and "Top Ten Business Books of All Time" by Xerox Corporation.

Two subsequent editions have been published in 1999 and 2006. Other books include *A Simpler Way*, co-authored with Myron Rogers (1996), *Turning to One Another: Simple Conversations to Restore Hope to the Future* (2002), and *Finding Our Way: Leadership for an Uncertain Time* (2005).

Margaret Wheatley has written a new book, *Perseverance* (2010), and has a new DVD, *Eight Fearless Questions*. She can be reached at *www.margaretwheatley.com*.

I want all leaders to ask themselves, Who do I choose to be for this time? This question signals that we have the opportunity to step forward beyond our traditional roles into a new and more courageous leadership. Instead of being focused on career success and advancement or performing our normal leadership functions, I want us to understand that the demands of this time require us to be rooted in our values, clear about our intentions, and available to people at a new depth. As everyone learns to cope with uncertainty, lost dreams and fear, we leaders need to step forward to enable people to get through this distressing time. We can only provide such leadership, whatever business we're in, by diving deep within ourselves and finding our true ground. No matter what our beliefs are, such a dive takes us into the realm of Spirit.

Turbulent times demand that we be grounded in our fundamental values. Leaders must look beyond the superficial and recognize that it is only our great human spirits that can get us through the most difficult life circumstances.

My poem "The True Professional" explores our role as leaders. I wrote it in tribute to Parker Palmer, one of the truly wise ones among us; one who has devoted his life to helping people reclaim a spiritual basis to their work. Parker wrote: "The true professional is a person whose action points beyond his or herself to that underlying reality, that hidden wholeness, on which we all can rely."[1] The true professional is a spiritual leader who realizes that we are part of something much greater than our petty personalities and egos, and that we work in the company of others who also are beautiful human spirits.

To compose this poem, I took lines from Parker Palmer's book *The Active Life*[2] and then let the lines change and morph and find new relationships with one another. This kind of poem is called a "found poem" because its key phrases are "found" in another's work. I wrote this poem for Parker, as partial thanks for all he has taught me over many years of friendship.

The True Professional

Illusion

Too much of our action is really reaction. Such doing does
not flow from free and independent hearts
but depends on external provocation.

Such doing does not flow
it depends on external provocation.

It does not come from our sense of
who we are and what we want to do, but from

our anxious reading of how others define us
    our anxious reading of how others define us
        our anxious reading of how others define us

and of what the world demands.

    When we react in this way we do not act humanly.

The true professional is one
who does not obscure grace
with illusions of technical prowess,
the true professional is one
who strips away all illusions to reveal

a reliable truth
a reliable truth in which
the human heart can rest.

    Can rest.

Unveil the illusions
    unveil the illusions that
        masquerade
the illusions that masquerade
as reality and reveal
    the reality
    behind the masks.

Catch the magician
deceiving us
    get a glimpse
        a glimpse of the
    truth behind the trick.

    A glimpse.

Contemplation happens anytime we get a glimpse of the
    truth.

Action

Action, like a sacrament,
is the visible form of an invisible spirit
an outward manifestation of
an inward power.

    An expressive act is not to achieve a goal outside
        myself
    but to express a conviction
    a leading, a truth that is within me.

An expressive act is one taken
because if I did not
if I did not
if I did not take it
I would be denying
my own insight, gift, nature.

Action, like a sacrament,
is the visible form of an invisible spirit
an outward manifestation of

an inward power. But as we act,
we not only express what is in us
and help give shape to the world.

We also receive what is outside us
and we reshape
        our inner selves.

When we act, the world acts back.

The world acts back
and we and the world,
we and the world are

co-created.

Right action is a process of birthing that cannot be
forced but only followed.

Surrender

When God's love for the world pierces our armor of
        fear
it is an awesome experience of calling and accountability.
When God's love pierces our armor of fear
it is awesome
it is awesome to be pierced by God
to be called to accountability
to be called by God's love
for the world.

The true professional is one
who does not obscure grace
with illusions of technical prowess,
the true professional is one
who strips away all illusions to reveal

a reliable truth in which
the human heart can rest.

Reveal a reliable truth.

Let our human hearts rest.

Good Business

Section III

Designing Spirited Organizations

Good Business

12. Becoming an Employer of Choice
Leigh Branham

Leigh Branham is the founder and CEO of Keeping the People, Inc., assisting organizations in developing strategies and practices for becoming better places to work. He is the author of *The Seven Hidden Reasons Employees Leave* (AMACOM Books, 2005) and *Keeping the People Who Keep You in Business* (AMACOM Books, 2000). He also publishes a free quarterly, *The Keeping the People Report.* He can be reached at *LB@keepingthepeople.com* or through his Web site, *www.keepingthepeople.com.*

Value, quality, service, honesty, integrity, caring, accountability, results, responsiveness. These are some of the words that appear most frequently in the company mission statements I've seen over the years. But, to me, the one word that encompasses all these professed values and that captures the essence of good business is *trust*.

Most businesses try and generally succeed in winning and maintaining our trust. But sadly, trust is missing at many

~~~

others, as the daily news reminds us. Bad business is all around us—from the greed and selfishness that produced the financial tsunami of 2008, to the Internet scams and spams, to shoddy workmanship, to the indifferent customer service that we are all too accustomed to encountering at restaurants or retail stores and in our "customer care" interactions with those in remote locations.

Trust implies several covenants with the customer: that services or products will be delivered as promised, that honesty will prevail instead of deceit or manipulation, that my time will not be wasted, and that company representatives will take responsibility for mistakes and failures to deliver. As Warren Buffet so succinctly stated, "Trust takes a lifetime to earn, but can be lost in seconds."

- I trust that when a painter says he will be at my house at 2 p.m., he will be there instead of calling two hours later to say that "something came up." I am amazed how few home service workers these days honor their promises to show up on time and respond to phone calls in a timely way.

- When I go to the post office, I still optimistically expect to be waited on in a timely fashion. I notice that on most days there are only two workers on duty even though there are five work stations. With eight to twelve people waiting patiently in line, it seems reasonable to expect that the two workers would move with a sense of urgency as they walk from the counter to the back room and return. Instead, they stroll at a glacial pace, sending the message loud and clear: "We don't care about your time."

• When I go to the doctor and have my blood pressure taken, the nurse almost never tells me what the reading is. I have to ask. Does she think I'm not interested, that it's none of my business since I'm only the patient?

There are many sins in the business world: selfishness, greed, deceit, indifference, laziness, irresponsibility and manipulation, to name a few. The one I find most personally aggravating, as you can probably tell, is indifference. That's because, as a customer, it is the sin I experience most often and most directly. At a very basic level, I trust and expect a business and its workers to care about giving good service and value. It is interesting to note that the American Society for Quality reports that 66 percent of all lost business can be traced back to a customer interaction with an indifferent employee.[1]

It seems to me that good business is all about the employee-customer interaction. That's where everything starts, where the rubber meets the road. And that's where the best companies—Southwest Airlines, Nordstrom, Ritz-Carlton, Whole Foods and many others—keep the focus. Yet the focus for leaders at many large public companies seems to be on stockholders, whom they regard as the primary stakeholders in the business. This translates into an almost single-minded focus on stock price and quarterly earnings reports, which, in turn, encourages managers to relentlessly push and pressure employees (instead of truly engage and motivate them) to meet short-term objectives, often with too few staff.

So what we have in many companies is a hierarchy, with stockholders at the top, being served by executives, being served by managers, being served by employees who serve the customers. This is upside down. The much more effective hierarchy has proven to be one with customer-contact employees at the top, being served by managers, being served by executives, with stockholders as the beneficiaries. For a fuller explanation of how this works to achieve business success, read Hal Rosenbluth's classic, *The Customer Comes Second*—the story of how he built the most successful business travel company in the world based on this model. A growing minority of today's employers have embraced the same mindset.

Most employers have, over the years, acclimated themselves to the status quo of having a largely unengaged workforce. Year after year, the Gallup Organization's employee engagement surveys indicate that only about 25 percent of America's workers are engaged, meaning they are willing to give their full (and often exceptional) discretionary effort on the job. Another 60 percent or so can be classified as "not engaged," meaning that on most days they are giving just enough effort, but not exceeding expectations or delighting customers. The remaining 15 percent or so are the "actively disengaged": your chronic underperformers, toxic underminers and professional victims—angry, resentful, larcenous, error- and accident-prone, capable of sabotage and destroying the morale of co-workers and relationships with customers. The estimated cost of the combined 75 percent of disengaged and unengaged workers to the U.S. economy is $400 to $500 billion per year.[2]

So the question I keep asking is why this clearly unacceptable situation has persisted over the years. I understand that the perfectibility of human nature is futile and that the disengaged will "always be with us," as will the poor. Many workers *are* lazy, *are* chronic whiners, feel excessively entitled to rewards without effort, have grossly unrealistic expectations, and are immune to motivational efforts. What intrigues me are the "employers of choice" I have studied since 1995 and the winning employers in the *Best-Places-to-Work* competitions (2003-present) whose cultures and practices I have had the privilege of analyzing for a book I co-authored.[3]

There are six we feature in our upcoming book: SAS Institute in North Carolina, Winchester Hospital in Massachusetts, Rackspace in San Antonio, Nalley Automotive in Atlanta, JDV Hospitality in San Francisco, and the Gaylord Palms Resort and Hotel in Orlando. Instead of having only about a quarter of their workers engaged, these "destination employers" typically are able to fully engage 60 percent or more of their employees and keep the number of actively disengaged to a minimum. So we were extremely interested in knowing what these special workplaces (and others like them) are doing to achieve employee engagement survey scores in the upper one percentile. We also carefully read their verbatim survey comments and found the following comment appearing again and again: "I feel so lucky to work here" (or words to that effect). The implication is clear: when employees feel they are the fortunate recipients of a superior work experience, they are more likely to give back in the form of greater effort and responsiveness to customers.

Our major finding was that there are six areas where the winning workplaces consistently outperform the nonwinners:

1. Their **senior leaders invest in employees** as assets to be served and developed, communicate more openly, and are more visible.

2. Their direct managers are selected and trained to be **good people managers** and are held accountable for engaging employees and for keeping employees' objectives aligned with those of the organization.

3. They create the conditions for **great teamwork** by eliminating "we-they" barriers and encouraging open sharing of information, constructive conflict and collaboration.

4. They **keep employees challenged and in jobs that fit** their talents and provide multiple opportunities for **learning, growth and development.**

5. They go out of their way to **recognize employee contributions** and demonstrate how much they **value all employees** in several ways—by listening and acting on employees' ideas, keeping them informed, and providing the right tools and resources.

6. They provide benefits and working conditions that demonstrate **genuine caring for employees' well-being.**

These are the drivers of employee engagement, the levers we have at our disposal to influence the willingness of employees to give back more of their limited energy and effort. The reaction I sometimes get when I present these engagement drivers in the talks I give is "So what else is new?" or "Yes, we already know these things are important," or "It's just common sense." My usual response is to point out just how uncommon common sense really is in common practice. It is human nature to want the easy button, the diet pill, the magic bullet. But the unpalatable truth is that leading and managing for optimum employee engagement is hard work, requiring real commitment to do the kinds of things that other employers are not willing to do.

The mystery to me is that despite knowing that these commonsense practices work, many leaders actually choose the self-defeating path by not using them. Leaders are only human too, after all. Until more leaders begin to transcend their narrow self-interest, let go of the need to overcontrol, and begin to see employees as their only true source of competitive advantage, they will have little hope of engaging those who trust in their leadership and serve their customers.

13. Spirit at Work
Val Kinjerski

Val Kinjerski, Ph.D., is a leading authority in the field of employee engagement and on the topic of spirit at work. An inspirational speaker, consultant and agent of change, she helps companies and organizations increase employee retention and boost productivity by re-igniting employees' love for their work. Her work and research have been featured in the press, presented at national and international conferences, and published in peer-reviewed journals. She has shown that spirit at work is not a pipe dream or the result of lucky circumstances. It is available to anyone; it can and should be fostered.

Dr. Kinjerski is the author of *Rethinking Your Work: Getting to the Heart of What Matters* and *Rethinking Your Work Guidebook: How to Get to the Heart of What Matters.* For more details, visit *www.kaizensolutions.org* or *www.rethinkingyourwork.com.*

$\mathbf{A}$ttracting, engaging and retaining talent has become a critical strategic need for today's businesses. Tighter budgets, a slowing economy and employee demand for more meaning and fulfillment at work have companies searching for new ways to be successful. Work as we know it has changed, and many companies are finding themselves at a critical crossroad.

Among the new approaches to increase an employee's meaningful experience at work and the success of the company is the promotion of *spirit at work*. I use this term to describe being fully engaged in our work. Feeling good about what we are doing and the contribution we are making. Sharing a common purpose and a sense of community with our colleagues. Connecting to something larger than ourselves, which has a positive effect on the way we work. For many, spirit at work has a mystical element to it—what some call a peak experience.

People with spirit at work possess a uniqueness. My research has found that people with high spirit at work are well-adjusted. They have a sense of inner harmony and positive energy. They are conscientious and spiritually inclined. Other researchers have found that people with spirit at work experienced increased job satisfaction, organizational commitment, work self-esteem and the lack of intention to quit their jobs. We know that these positive work attitudes are associated with lower absenteeism and turnover and improved job performance. Therefore, it makes sense that spirit at work would also be related to lower absenteeism and turnover and improved job performance. And it is!

I would like to share the results of a study that tested the impact of a spirit-at-work program on employees and the workplace. Based on my research and experience as a consultant, I created and delivered a program that focused on developing and enhancing spirit at work. I delivered this program through organizational workshops. Although the workshop evaluations were very positive, I wanted to learn if participants' spirit at work really increased and was sustained. Did the spirit-at-work program impact work-related attitudes? Did it make any difference in employee retention? What about customer service?

In conjunction with the University of Alberta, I designed a study to find the answers to these questions. Two similar groups from different worksites within a large organization agreed to participate. In addition to a heavy workload and difficult clients, the first group experienced poor morale, difficult staff relationships and communication concerns. This group was selected to attend the spirit-at-work program. The second group acted as a comparison group and did not attend any sessions.

To see if there were any differences that could be attributed to the spirit-at-work program, both groups completed questionnaires prior to and after completion of the program. Employees and team leaders were also provided with the opportunity to comment on their experiences after the program was completed.

The Spirit-at-Work Program
The spirit-at-work program consisted of a one-day workshop supplemented by eight weekly one-hour booster ses-

sions. The workshop focused on spirit at work—what it is, personal strategies that foster it, and organizational conditions which cultivate it. Employees were led through a variety of discussions and exercises that culminated in the creation of personal action plans to enhance their spirit at work. My earlier research showed that the creation of spirit at work is a shared responsibility—shared between the employee and the employer. So there was some time during the program spent discussing the organizational conditions that foster spirit at work, such as inspired leadership, a sense of community, opportunity for personal fulfillment, and a positive workplace culture. However, the emphasis was on what individuals could do to cultivate their spirit at work and contribute to an environment that supported spirit at work, regardless of position or level. Personal strategies such as being on purpose, being of service, appreciating self and others, and self-care were explored individually and in small groups.

After the workshop, employees attended one of several booster sessions offered weekly. The intent of the booster sessions was to support employees' efforts to enhance their spirit at work and to promote a sense of team. Building on the workshop and responding to participant requests, topics for the booster sessions included mindfulness, the power of positive thoughts, strengthening relationships through communication (reducing gossip), and cultivating a spiritual life. Additional topics covered were developing a sense of community, dealing with difficult situations, and creating time for fun and celebrations. Each session followed a format that began with a centering exercise, check-in, presentation and application of the topic. They closed with a word of hope.

The Business Case

Participation in the program was enough to reduce absenteeism by 60 percent and turnover by 75 percent. For the group attending the program, spirit at work increased by 11 percent; as it increased, so, too, did positive work-related attitudes. The group saw a 23 percent increase in teamwork, a 10 percent hike in job satisfaction and a 17 percent jump in workplace morale. Both organizational commitment and overall organizational culture improved by 13 percent. As expected, the site not participating in the program did not experience any of these results. On the contrary, they saw an increase in employee turnover.[1]

Focus groups with employees and team leaders affirmed that the spirit-at-work program was a success. Participants of the program felt an improvement in overall morale and teamwork, became aware of their personal growth and development, and could see a more positive focus on service. Here is what they had to say.

Morale and Teamwork Improved

Morale on the unit immediately improved. A team leader said, "We now know how to communicate with one another, how to love one another, and how to respect one another." Realizing the importance of their work, staff came to recognize that they were all needed to make the unit a success. They talked about being more supportive of each another and observed one another helping more. Early in the program, a team leader said, "I saw staff working together, without complaints. I saw teamwork." One employee summed up the experience when he said, "I cannot believe how, in such a short period of time, we could come together as a group."

Staff were more considerate, friendlier and kinder towards co-workers. As their understanding of each other increased, so did their respect for each other and their differences. One leader said, "I have seen changes on the floor. Staff are having fun, expressing more joy, sharing jokes, and showing respect to each other." Communication was more open, honest, respectful and positive. Co-workers listened more. They shared more information. Gossip decreased.

Positive attitudes increased and negativity among co-workers decreased. One participant said, "I am more open ... taking more responsibility ... not blaming others." They spoke of "making conscious choices" to be positive and "having a 'just do it' attitude." Many staff adopted an attitude of turning difficult situations into positive ones by "turning lemons into lemonade."

Personal Growth and Development Were Enhanced

Employees reported being "happier and more excited to go to work" because colleagues were happier and it was less stressful to be at work. Before the program, they said that it was "tense" on the floor, no one was "happy," and there was "a lot of gossip." Co-workers were "doing their own stuff" and "not helping each other." This all changed after attending the program. For example, one person said, "I have this new vitality at work, and I just want to make it better." As an added benefit, participants spoke about being able to transfer what they learned to their family and their community.

A Focus on Service Increased

A key component of the program is helping employees appreciate that all work is about serving others. An equally important element is assisting employees to uncover the deeper meaning underlying their particular work. Upon gaining a clearer understanding of this, they reported being "kinder," "more forgiving" and "more appreciative" of their clients. It didn't take long before they knew they were making a difference because of the positive feedback received in response to their changed behaviors. For example, one person said, "I noticed that a lady who is generally depressed gave me a bright smile today because of the things I said. I knew I made a difference." Employees from different sections began working together for the overall good. A supervisor noticed "others doing extras and hearing 'thank you' from clients." She said that it quickly became clear that "we were serving others." One employee's comment was indicative of the transformation experienced by many: "I have meaning in my work. I am not just working for money. I now know that my work is important. I work from the heart."

The Promise of Spirit at Work

This study confirms what many forward-thinking leaders already know. When we get to the heart of what matters about our work, when we feel the work we are doing is important, and we can see how we make a difference in the lives of others, everything changes—for the employee, the organization and the people being served. Not only do employees experience increased spirit at work, they are more satisfied with and committed to their work and organization. They connect with the deeper purpose underlying their work and focus on making a difference. The culture of the organization shifts. In particular, a shared sense of purpose emerges, a strong sense of team develops, and morale is heightened. All this leads to employees who want to stay and contribute. For businesses, this translates into enhanced engagement, increased retention and improved customer service—key elements to productivity.

In order to attract, engage and maintain employees, work itself must be understood to be rewarding and fulfilling. All work has value. All work matters. All work provides opportunities to make a contribution. A major thrust of the spirit-at-work program is assisting employees to appreciate the importance of their particular contribution by uncovering the meaning and deeper purpose of their work—by getting to the heart of what matters.

This deeper purpose is fulfilled by serving: serving others or serving a cause. It is through service that employees make a contribution, and that is where the meaning and fulfillment come from. Helping them to see their work as an "act of service" changes their view of work and positively impacts how they work. Adopting the approach of people with high spirit at work—"It is not about me, it is about them: the customer, client, patient"—leads to a changed attitude and positive results for the employee, the organization and the customer. Relationships are key to staff engagement and retention. A sense of community—knowing that we all belong and have a shared purpose—is critical to the development of spirit at work and is cultivated by supporting relationships. Bringing together staff on the same team and at all levels provides opportunities to support others in their work and to understand challenges faced by different roles. It also creates an environment for all employees to express appreciation for one another, which goes a long way toward developing a sense of team.

Spirit at work has practical and profitable implications for the workplace. Implementing a spirit-at-work program is a relatively inexpensive, but powerful, way to increase the organizational commitment and work satisfaction of employees. Increasing spirit at work improves organizational culture, reduces turnover and absenteeism while improving quality of service. For organizations wanting to build a competitive advantage through a highly engaged and committed workforce, the creation of spirit at work is critical.

These research results pave the way for program enhancements to foster spirit at work in the workplace. Attention to the deeper meaning underlying work, a focus on service, encouragement of relationships and teamwork among all staff, facilitation of personal responsibility to effect positive change within individuals and the organization, expression of appreciation towards colleagues, and the promotion of positive thought and communication will go a long way towards improving working conditions and assuring business success in any organization.

14. The Power of a Values-Based Culture

Susan Mundy Beck

Susan Mundy Beck is the chief operating officer at the Association of Unity Churches International. In this position, she facilitates strategic planning efforts and coordinates activities of the vice presidents to ensure completion of all plans and projects in support of Unity ministries worldwide. Formerly the executive director of the HearthStone Global Foundation in Omaha, Nebraska, she initiated and managed several significant global projects, including efforts to promote large-scale conscious transformation within nations, including Israel, and within businesses, other organizations and communities. Susan served 24 years as an Air Force officer and retired in 2001 from the Office of the Secretary of the Air Force in the Pentagon after achieving the rank of colonel.

When thinking about the essence of good business, there are many topics that immediately come to mind.

III — Designing Spirited Organizations

Numerous books have been written about new techniques and tools, many of which are popular for a time, but they fade away when the next new book comes along. These books all seem to guarantee success if we will just implement their concepts. There is a principle that stands the test of time. Dr. Maria Nemeth, founder of the Academy for Coaching Excellence and author of *Mastering Life's Energies*, teaches that the essence of success for any organization or individual is doing everything with great *clarity* and *focus*. She declares that clarity and focus yield ease and grace in whatever we do.[1] She is right, of course. Whenever we get clear about what we want to do and give it our close attention or focus, we will have ease and grace in the doing because we are totally aligned with and present to it.

Undoubtedly, there are many aspects of business or other organizations in which we could gain clarity and on which we might focus, but there is one essential aspect at the heart of any organization that warrants greater clarity and focus: its core values. This is a simple thing, but it often gets overlooked for more complex organizational interventions.

When the core values within any organization are made explicit and practiced by the individuals within the organization, there is a level of cultural coherence not often seen in organizations. Not only is this coherence experienced by the leadership and employees/associates within the business, it is experienced by the customers, clients, shareholders and other stakeholders.

There is much research indicating that organizations that live their core values experience solid bottom-line success and longevity. In her book *Value Shift*, Lynn Sharp Paine, former John G. McLean Professor at the Harvard Business School, convincingly links the alignment and practice of core values with outstanding financial results. She lists five reasons chief executive officers embrace core values. These reasons relate to risk management, organizational functioning, market positioning, civic positioning, and just because it is the right thing to do, as they recognize the inherent worth of values within the organization.[2] Several other studies have proven that a main factor in organizational longevity is establishment of a strong, positive, values-driven culture.

My own experience indicates that organizations where there is alignment with and focus on core values enjoy more than just financial results; they experience greater customer satisfaction, along with employee fulfillment and retention as well. I experienced this directly while working for a large home-building company for which I was the director of organizational development. The company's customer survey results (performed by an independent agency) repeatedly indicated a high degree of satisfaction, not only with the home-building experience, but also in dealing with the company's associates (who were all practicing the company's core values). Further, because of the work environment, associate turnover was very low throughout the time I was employed there. When asked why they stayed in the company, associates related stories about the values-based culture and the trust and commitment to the company's mission and aims that it engendered.

What are core values and why focus on them?

In looking at the concept of making core values explicit in organizations and actually practicing them, there is one expert who stands out because he has pioneered much work on the subject. In his books, which I highly recommend, *Liberating the Corporate Soul: Building a Visionary Organization* (1998) and *Building a Values-Driven Organization: A Whole System Approach* (2006), Richard Barrett discusses why core values are important.

Essentially, he has found that "the purpose of establishing a set of values is to create a code of behavior that builds a cohesive culture and supports the [organization's] vision and mission."[3] In such a culture, the values become "rules" not only for living and working within the organization, but especially for decision-making. Values are "deeply-held beliefs that a certain way of being or a certain outcome is preferable to another."[4]

In making their values explicit, organizations must be very clear about the actions and behaviors that will demonstrate the values both within the organization and externally. Then, to "walk the talk," an organization and its people must be totally congruent with their values by continuously practicing these organizational actions and behaviors. According to Richard, "Values 'talk.' Behaviors 'walk.'"[5]

Once the organization is clear about its values and how to walk the talk, people within the organization will come to understand what is expected of them. As individuals and teams practice the values daily and experience the benefits in terms of greater trust, cohesion and unity, they fully embrace the values and everyone becomes "mutually accountable." Ultimately, the values create an environment within which everyone can operate with "responsible freedom."[6]

Richard's work with organizations across the globe indicates that "strong [organizations] are characterized by sincere friendliness and the ability to pursue shared objectives quickly and efficiently. The strength of a community [organization] depends on the commitment of its individual members to live by the shared values—no exception for leaders or managers."[7] In fact, if anything, those in leadership positions are the key to creating a strong, values-based culture. The leaders must be role models for the values in everything they do to support the full integration of the values throughout the organization.

So core values essentially serve three purposes: they provide guidelines for corporate/organizational and individual behaviors; they provide direction for decision-making; and they support the organization in creating a culture that will enable it to actualize its mission and vision of success.

Core Values: Guidelines for Organizational and Individual Behaviors

When I consult with organizations that want to consciously and intentionally shape their culture and design their future together, I start by supporting them in making their core values explicit. To do this, it is important to not just work with the top leadership, but to engage people at all levels of the organization, as they will all be living the core values together.

While organizations may want to choose particular values and aspire to practice them, I have learned through my work that certain positive core qualities or values are already at the heart of every organization; they are implicit within the organization. Organizations are often more successful in bringing these core values into the light of understanding and intentionally practicing them, than in aspiring to "be" something they are not.

Some examples of core values follow:

- Acceptance
- Authenticity
- Creativity
- Compassion
- Courage
- Flexibility
- Generosity
- Inclusion

- Innovation
- Integrity
- Open-mindedness
- Stewardship
- Service
- Transparency
- Trust
- Honesty

There are many more that can be listed. These examples are intended to indicate some positive qualities or "ways of being" (values) that may be at the core of an organization. An important distinction to note is that core values don't indicate what the organization values (externally), but rather "who" the organization is at its core (internally). This is the key to understanding core values.

So it is important to start by discerning the values the organization has at its core and then bring them into conscious practice to create a strong, positive, values-based organizational culture. There are several ways to make the core values explicit. One is for the organization to complete an online cultural values assessment, such as the one offered by the Barrett Values Centre (*www.valuescentre.com*). If that is not possible, another way is to create an organizational discovery process based on the use of appreciative inquiry techniques. This will help the organization determine what core values are already present so they may be practiced more intentionally within and outside the organization. One thing to keep in mind is that three to five core values are sufficient. If there are too many, they become hard for people to remember and practice.

Once the core values are discerned, the task of fully developing them begins. This work should engage not only the leadership but some of the associates of the organization, since everyone must align with the core values to create a strong, powerful, values-based culture. In this work, it is important to first define what is meant by each core value— one sentence each. For example, for the core value of integrity, a one-sentence definition might be "We are ethical in all our actions and honor the commitments we make." It is important to start with the word *we* so these definitions can be integrated into the organization and affirmed together.

The next step is to develop organizational actions that will demonstrate the core values on an organizational level, as well as individual behavior statements. This will support the organization in implementing and integrating the core values and enable people in the organization to walk the talk. An example of organizational actions for the core value of integrity might be "[Name of organization] is truthful in all product advertising." Another might be "[Name of the organization] is forthright in all communications with stakeholders." For an individual behavior relating to the core value of integrity, we might see "I always do as I say I will. I keep my word."

To fully develop core values, the final "spreadsheet" should include a definition for each core value (starting with "We"); the three or four organizational actions that will be taken to demonstrate each value; and three behaviors for each value that individual employees/associates will practice to walk the talk (individual behaviors).

Once this work is done, the organization must take whatever time is needed to thoroughly integrate the core values into the organization and into the awareness and practice of the leadership and employees/associates. The ways of doing this are limited only by the creativity of the organization and its people. Overall, if the employees/associates participate in creating the core values while understanding the need for them and they design creative ways to implement them into their daily routine, they will be more likely to support their integration.

At the home-building company I mentioned earlier, the associates had an extensive understanding and practice of the core values. Everyone in the company knew the core values by heart and could explain how they were walking the talk. Newcomers were given a small card containing the values, and they learned them quickly because of the consistent focus on them. When I first came into the company, it was clear that their culture was different, and I soon figured out why: the alignment with and practice of the company's five core values were central to our way of being. They were palpable and definitely influenced the way we were with each other and with our customers. There was no question; our core values made a difference.

Core Values: Direction for Decision-Making

An organization's core values, along with its mission, should be closely considered in decision-making. This means that decisions that are made will be in alignment with the organization's reason for and way of being. When leaders and others use core values for decision-making, decisions almost "make themselves" at times, and they will be carried out more easily and successfully because they are in alignment with the actions and practices associated with the core values.

Again, citing my experience in the home-building company, decisions were always made with the core values and mission in mind. In fact, the core values and their definition statements were recited at the beginning of every meeting; the word *every* is no exaggeration. Of course, there were many meetings every day, and the core values were recited in the beginning of each one to set the "arena" in which the meeting took place. Any discussions that happened and decisions that were made after setting the arena were always in accord with the core values.

I remember a time when the financial well-being of the company could have been very negatively affected by a decision that looked like it had to be made to stay in alignment with our core values. The company's advertising on appliance efficiency was being questioned by a customer. The owner, president and CEO of the company, a man for whom the core values were of utmost importance, wanted to make sure that what we delivered to our customers was in alignment with our advertising, as integrity was one of our core values. Fortunately, some information came to light that showed that that we actually were in integrity in our advertising. If this had not happened, we might have had to take a remedy that would have had a serious financial impact on the company. Not all organizations are that conscientious about living their core values. But, according to the research, the most successful ones are.

Core Values: Support for Actualizing the Mission and Achieving the Vision

Organizations have a greater ability to pursue shared objectives quickly and efficiently when there is a strong, positive, values-based culture in an organization; when the people are in alignment with the core values, they create a culture that supports speed and efficiency. They know how they can expect their colleagues to be and what they can count upon each other to do; therefore, they work more efficiently and effectively together. This supports achievement of the organization's mission and vision.

Closing Thoughts

The principle that clarity and focus bring about ease and grace is a thread that runs through this chapter. Whatever we focus on expands. The concept of consistency or coherency is the magnifying effect of one factor upon another. It is the clarity and consistency of focus on core values that, over time, establishes a strong, positive, values-based culture. This culture reinforces the other parts of the organization to form an integrated whole that is much more powerful than the sum of the parts. It is only through this clarity and focus over time that an organization and its people can achieve maximum results.

15. Good Business in Tough Economic Times

Margaret Benefiel and Debora Jackson

Margaret Benefiel, Ph.D., teaches at Andover Newton Theological School in Boston and at the Milltown Institute in Dublin, Ireland. CEO of ExecutiveSoul.com, Dr. Benefiel also has served as chair of the Academy of Management's Management Spirituality and Religion Group. More than 500 executives, managers and other leaders have participated in her seminars and courses. She is the author of *Soul at Work: Spiritual Leadership in Organizations* (2005) and *The Soul of a Leader: Finding Your Path to Success and Fulfillment* (2008) and has also written for *The Leadership Quarterly, Management Communication Quarterly, Managerial Finance, Journal of Organizational Change Management, Organization, Personal Excellence, America, Presence, The Way, Studies in Spirituality, Radical Grace* and *Faith at Work.*

Debora Jackson was the CIO and COO of SmartEnergy, Inc.,
managing director for Avicon, regional director of Professional
Services for Sherpa Corporation, and director of delivery at
Sapient Corporation. She founded The Renewal Group, a con-
sultancy focused on revitalizing organizations after downsizing
and on maximizing employee engagement. Debora authored
the article "Seven Strategies for Revitalization After Downsizing"
and provided independent consulting services to organizations
facing restructuring, designing and implementing strategies to
foster growth within the organizations. Debora is also a spiritual
leader. She is an ordained member of the clergy and senior
pastor of the First Baptist Church in Needham, Massachusetts.

Can good business be sustained in tough economic times?
Are the tenets of good business different in good times
than in bad? We maintain that the tenets of good business
remain the same, in good times and in bad, and that there is
a more compelling need to utilize them during the difficult
times. When businesses face tough times, leaders, managers
and employees all tend to withdraw. In tough times, many
co-workers become reticent and inward-focused. The challenge in tough times is to remain open to the opportunities,
prepared for the possibilities, with the expectation that such
openness will positively affect the organization. How a busi-

ness faces tough times forms the foundation for its future. We will discuss five tenets of good business and show how they play out in tough economic times, with a focus on the case for layoffs—when layoffs are necessary and how can they be done in a way consistent with good business.

Five Tenets of Good Business

During tough economic times, it is critical that organizations work to strengthen relationships, creating and maintaining connection with employees. The anxiety of recession manifests itself in the demeanor of the workforce. Such stress can cause employees to be closed-off and ambivalent. When the stresses of the environment bear down to pull relationships apart, leaders must work to overcome those stresses and re-ignite a sense of collegiality and community.

The first tenet of good business is to create opportunities for intentional relationship-building. This may be as simple as utilizing the first few minutes of a meeting for "check-in," giving employees an opportunity to express themselves. Through intentional connection, people come together more meaningfully and, in doing so, strengthen the bonds of relationship.

For clients and trading partners, the same practices can be employed. Executives and managers can take time to know their clients personally and not just professionally. Managers might ask clients what they need and how they might alleviate stress for them in tough times.

The second tenet of good business is honest self-examination. For individuals, the questions are: "Is your work sustaining you or are you on a path to burnout? Are you bringing your best self to work or are you simply going through the motions?" Questions like these are especially important to ask in tough times so that individuals can discern whether they are part of the problem or part of the solution.

For the organization as a whole, the questions are: "Do our business practices maximize organizational efficiency? Do our structures and processes allow people to bring their best selves to work?"

The third tenet of good business is to courageously make necessary changes. When individuals, for example, recognize that they are not bringing their best selves to their work, they and their employer need to face that reality and determine what changes need to occur. Are changes needed in the employee or in the position? Is it time for the employee to transition out of the job? When, on the organizational level, it becomes clear that structures and processes are not facilitating people being their best selves at work, it is time to change those structures and processes.

The fourth tenet of good business is to plan a way forward. Good businesses give themselves permission to think without constraints, thus creating a renewed sense of hope and optimism for the future.

Finally, the fifth tenet of good business is to set a tactical course, to consider the steps that are required to bring the strategic plan to fruition. Through consultation within the organization, writing up a step-by-step action plan, and then taking action, the plan can begin to become a reality.

Layoffs

Following these five tenets in tough times does not guarantee that everything will be easy. Sometimes only one conclusion can be drawn: layoffs are necessary.

The feelings that often arise when the topic of layoffs is broached in an organization are fear, anger, despair, abandonment and betrayal. Layoffs stir up in individuals and organizations the deepest, darkest emotions. Are "good" layoffs possible? Can "good business" and layoffs go together?

For employer and employee alike, layoffs are the most dreaded implication of a recession. Because layoffs are dreaded, employers often do not face the necessity of layoffs until the last possible moment, and as a result, do not carefully think through how to best implement them, when they do become necessary, to minimize damage to individuals and to the organization.

Consequently, layoffs leave in their wake not only wounded former employees but also shell-shocked remaining employees, who are now expected to do more with less. Furthermore, the remaining employees get the message that they shouldn't have any negative emotions; they should be feeling full of gratitude toward their employers because they still have their jobs.

Yet the remaining employees often suffer the most. While laid-off employees may be recipients of counseling, job training and job placement assistance, the remaining employees are expected to soldier on with no extra support. They are experiencing grief from the sudden loss of co-workers with whom they shared daily work for years, even decades. They are experiencing fear, wondering when the other shoe will drop and they, too, will be let go. They are experiencing "survivor guilt," wondering why they still have jobs while their equally or better-qualified colleagues do not. They are experiencing exhaustion, both emotional and physical, from what they have been through in the organizational downsizing and from the heavier workload placed upon them with no end in sight.

Because of this emotional overload, the remaining employees can't work to capacity. Morale plummets. Teamwork suffers. Malaise sets in across the organization.

Can layoffs be done in a way that honors and respects the remaining employees? Can they be done in a way that keeps the life and energy of the organization alive? Can they be done in such a way that the remaining employees bring their full commitment and motivation to work at a time when the company most needs them to be their best selves?

Here are seven strategies for revitalizing individuals and organizations.

Strategy 1: Communicate clearly. Good communication is key to successful revitalization. Executives and managers need to be transparent, to be sensitive, honest and clear. Employees are much more likely to want to give their best to the company when they know they are being told the truth. Employees are not naïve. They hear the news. They can read the handwriting on the wall. When information is withheld, rumors fly. When they receive regular, honest reports of how leaders are addressing the challenges before them, employees can relax and devote their energies to their work. Rumors will die out.

Strategy 2: Develop an employee support plan. Remaining employees need to know that they are more than just cogs in a machine, a machine that is now expected to do more with less. They need to know that they are valued for the gifts and skills they bring to the organization. Different employees will respond differently after downsizing and thus need different kinds of support. Some might need a brief separation from the company. Others will need to talk about the layoffs and their response. Others will respond by reassessing their career goals and how those fit with the company. Leaders need to be prepared for all these responses and to support employees however they respond. Offering employees career planning is key at this stage. Leaders can help employees articulate their desires and goals and focus on personal growth and development, which will re-energize employees.

Strategy 3: Acknowledge feelings. Remaining employees need to know that their emotional needs as human beings will be acknowledged and respected at this difficult time. If feelings are not allowed expression, employees remain stuck in grief and depression and become ineffective at work. Providing an organizationwide opportunity to grieve can help employees move through their feelings. Holding a wake is one such grieving opportunity. At a wake, the remaining employees can mourn the downsizing and, at the same time, celebrate the past accomplishments of laid-off employees.

Holding facilitated conversations can also provide an opportunity for employees to express their feelings and move through their grief. In a facilitated conversation, employees realize that their feelings are normal, that other employees are experiencing similar feelings, and that they will indeed come through to the other side.

Strategy 4: Reestablish focus. Once leaders have helped employees acknowledge their feelings and move through the grieving process, they can begin to re-establish focus on immediate tasks. At this stage the leadership and employees can work together to identify the immediate, high-priority tasks that need to be done. By identifying together which tasks are most important, leadership can help to rebuild trust. Furthermore, by following through and focusing only on those tasks deemed most important, the leadership demonstrates to the remaining employees that they don't expect that everything that was previously accomplished can be accomplished with a reduced staff.

Strategy 5: Develop a plan. The organizational plan provides hope for employees as it focuses on the future. An organizational plan that takes seriously employee input and feedback benefits from shared wisdom and assures employees that their perspectives are valued.

Strategy 6: Align roles and goals. At this juncture, managers and employees can work together to align employee career goals with the organizational plan. Both the organization and the employee will benefit from this alignment as they gain a clearer sense of how their missions can work synergistically.

Strategy 7: Establish metrics to measure success. This strategy allows the organization to measure how it is functioning with regard to stated goals to ensure expected performance. To make measurement possible, the organization can choose appropriate metrics, such as employee satisfaction scores or customer survey results.

These seven strategies can be used in any company after layoffs, tailored, of course, to the particular culture of the company. The remaining employees need at least as much attention as those laid off. By paying attention to the needs of the remaining employees after a layoff, an organization can experience revitalization and can return to working at full capacity.

Conclusion

Good business is about companies following the same tenets for sustaining a business in tough economic times as they do in good times. Creating and maintaining relational connections provides the impetus that allows a company to operate in strength and hope. It is this kind of intentional relationship-building that galvanizes teams, organizations and even clients into a cohesive unit that is able to look beyond the tough times with optimism and energy.

Furthermore, when necessary, good business is also about being able to conduct layoffs in ways that allow employees and organizations to honor the past, reflect on the present and set a course for future. Such a process prepares the organizational soil for new growth and new opportunities to be seized by revitalized employees who are engaged and ready.

Creating an organization that is optimistic, energetic, engaged and ready—that is good business.

Section IV

Conscious Contributors

16. The Power of Choice
Jim Bearden

Jim Bearden is an internationally recognized speaker and
consultant whose expertise is in leadership, teamwork and
personal accountability. His goal is to help people awaken to the
relationship between personal accountability and success. He is
the author of *The Relentless Search for Better Ways*, 2006.

*"One afternoon in July 1968, the theoretical phase
of my marine training ended and the practical phase
began—with a bang!"*
—The Relentless Search for Better
Ways, Jim Bearden, 2006

They Came in the Evening

Late in the afternoon of my 12th day as a marine rifle platoon
commander in Vietnam, my platoon came under attack by
a North Vietnamese unit intent on overrunning our isolated hilltop position. In the first few moments of the attack, the other
officers in our rifle company (three platoons) went down, leaving me in command. In a matter of minutes, I'd gone from being
the junior officer to being the commanding officer.

That experience provided me with an excellent—but difficult—opportunity to learn some basic truths about life:

1. The people, situations and circumstances—the eternal factors—in our lives change.

2. Some of those changes occur unexpectedly and affect us negatively; setbacks are not just possible or probable, they are *inevitable.*

3. The choices we make *about* the setbacks we encounter are more powerful—have more impact on us—than the setbacks themselves.

Of those three truths, the third one has become the basis for my work as a speaker, writer, trainer and facilitator. It reflects my conviction that winning, in a changing world, is an inside-out process.

Mental and Mechanical

Our responses to setbacks, the choices we make about them, fall into two categories: mental and mechanical. Since most people focus exclusively on the latter, let's start there. Our mechanical choices are the things we do, the actions we take, after encountering setbacks. Are our mechanical choices important? Of course they are. Can we improve the actions we take in response to setbacks? Again, the answer is yes. But here's something to consider when seeking to make such improvements. Our mechanical choices, the things we do to deal with the setbacks we encounter, are dramatically affected—even determined—by that other category, the mental choices we make.

What that means is that in order to improve the actions we take in response to setbacks (our mechanical choices), we must be willing to acknowledge and improve the mental choices we make *about* those setbacks. Since our mental choices are based on our perspective, let's begin by taking a look at the perspective we're currently using to process the outside factors in our lives, including the setbacks we encounter.

A Tale of Two Perspectives

When I ask audiences to share their thoughts about what perspective is, the most common responses are variations of "responsibility." That's a good starting point, but for me, it doesn't really capture the scope of what perspective is or how it plays out in our lives.

I believe perspective is the place in mind from where we not only perceive (gather information) but also process (assign meanings to) what we see/hear. For example, what does it mean to be 60? I'm sure you'll agree that it pretty much depends on where you're "looking at 60 from." Teenagers can be counted on to assign different meanings than will people who have actually reached that milestone. Even though both groups (teenagers and boomers) are looking at the same number used in the same context, they'll assign totally different meanings, based on their perspectives, or "where they're looking at 60 from" (pardon the grammar).

That same phenomenon applies to setbacks. People assign different meanings to them based on their perspectives. Using their different perspectives, they make different mental choices, and those mental choices will lead them to take different actions. The current economic downturn provides opportunities to see some of the different mechanical choices that people make about setbacks. Some "hunker, wait and hope" for conditions to improve. Others look for ways to win, regardless of the hands they're dealt. Those different responses to the same outside factor (the economy) are manifestations of the two most common perspectives people use to process setbacks: *victimhood* and *accountability*.

Victimhood

Perspective begins with belief, and here's the belief that underlies victimhood: *My feelings are the emotional consequences of the outside factors in my life.* I want you to think about that for a minute. What I'm suggesting is that most people believe (not think or suspect, but *believe*) that their feelings are caused by the people, situations and circumstances in their lives. Having trouble accepting that? Here's a question for you to ponder: Can you think of people in your life who upset you? If so, then you obviously believe that those people and their behavior somehow *create* your feelings.

Armed with that belief, most people establish criteria that must be met in order for them to experience positive feelings, "rules" for their happiness, the things that must or must not happen "out there" in order for them to be happy. Whether they call them pet peeves, attachments, aversions, demands or expectations doesn't matter. What does matter is that somewhere along the way most people have become convinced that positive feelings are situational phenomena, that emotionally they are at the mercy of outside factors. In short, they've relegated themselves to the status of victims since most of their rules apply to outside factors over which they have absolutely no control.

And what sort of choices do victims make when (not if) their rules are violated? The answer is obvious; victims make victim choices. They blame their suffering on the outside factors, they wallow in those feelings, using their thoughts about their feelings and about the setbacks to intensify and prolong the drama and their suffering. They feed their negative feelings with their thoughts, the mental choices they make, all the while overlooking—even denying—the role they've played in creating, intensifying and prolonging those feelings.

Let me close our discussion of victimhood with this observation: *All "professional victims" are volunteers.* We can't be drafted into victimhood; it is a choice we make. More accurately, it is a culmination of several choices we've made, beginning with the underlying belief that supports it. Happily, there is an alternative perspective for processing the outside factors in our lives. That alternative is accountability.

Accountability

Accountability, like victimhood, is based on an underlying belief. Victimhood is based on the mistaken belief that our feelings are the emotional consequences of the outside factors in our lives. The belief that supports accountability is more than just a belief; it is a truth, and it goes like this: *My feelings are the emotional consequences of the mental choices I make, including the mental choices I make about the outside factors in my life.*

Does that mean that the outside factors don't matter, that setbacks don't have any impact on us? Of course not. What it does mean is that our mental choices about the setbacks we encounter will do one of two things. They will either compound or mitigate the negative impact those setbacks have on us.

Armed with this belief about the creative power of their thoughts (the mental choices they make), consciously accountable folks engage in a mental training process. Having acknowledged the creative power of their thoughts (becoming conscious of their inherent accountability), they develop the mental discipline necessary to acknowledge and improve the mental choices they make.

Upgrading their "rules" to preferences is one phase of that mental training process, a process that is really quite simple, but one that does require vigilance. Here are the steps in this phase of that process:

1. Catch yourself "bummed out" (experiencing negative feelings, e.g., fear or anger).

2. Step back mentally from the feelings (stop identifying with them, take a temporary time out from your suffering).

3. Just observe—pay attention to—your thoughts about the situation you've encountered, the one you've held accountable for your being bummed out. Don't be judgmental; don't create more suffering about the thoughts you were having; just observe them.

4. That's it. Nothing else is required. When you stop feeding your negative feelings with the unconscious

thoughts you were running, those negative feelings will subside.

Please note that when you fall back into your "autopilot" mode (stop observing your thoughts), they will probably begin creating more drama (negative emotional consequences). Pay attention to your feelings, and when you catch yourself bummed out again, simply repeat the process.

Perseverance is essential, and it will pay off in two ways. In the early stage of your mental training process, you will reduce the intensity and duration of your self-induced suffering (the victim choices you make about the setbacks you encounter). In the latter stage, you'll find yourself making fewer victim choices regardless of the hands you're dealt. The intensity and duration of your suffering will not be an issue *since you'll be creating less suffering.* Not only will you experience better feelings, you'll also improve your effectiveness at dealing with the outside factors in your life, including the inevitable setbacks you encounter.

Victims make victim choices about setbacks; they blame the setbacks for the negative feelings they're experiencing, and they unconsciously intensify and prolong their self-imposed suffering. Consciously accountable people make accountable choices about the setbacks they encounter. Instead of blaming and wallowing, they *get over it and get on with it.*

Get Over It

Consciously accountable people do not engage in denial. "Ignore and hope" is not a strategy they employ for dealing with setbacks. They acknowledge the setbacks they encounter and the impact those setbacks have on them and on their efforts to achieve and sustain success. Consciously accountable people don't engage in victim behavior, but they still care about the outside factors they encounter. So when those outside factors affect them negatively, consciously accountable people will do some *appropriate, rational grieving*.

Disappointment is a good example of an appropriate, rational form of grieving. It is an emotion that can easily translate into behavior for dealing with setbacks. Devastation, on the other hand, is a bit over the top. People who are devastated are simply too busy being devastated (wallowing) to do much of anything about the setbacks they've used to devastate themselves. Remember: *All professional victims are volunteers.*

Get on With It

There are three "time zones" for the mental choices we make: the past, the present and the future. Professional victims seem to focus almost exclusively on the dead past (wallowing by reliving setbacks and continuing to feed their negative feelings) and the imagined future (convincing themselves that negative past events will be repeated). Consciously accountable people acknowledge past setbacks; do appropriate, rational grieving; determine what they can do now (in the present); and then they do it. And that brings me back to where I began, on a hill, a long way from home.

The Morning After

Early in the morning of my 13th day in Vietnam, after a long night of fighting to hold our hilltop position, I was preparing to lead a patrol to ensure that the area around our perimeter was secure and that the surviving North Vietnamese soldiers had withdrawn. The marines who would be accompanying me on the patrol were checking each other's gear while I pored over my map of the terrain we would be traversing.

Apparently my facial expression revealed the shock and sadness I felt about the casualties we'd taken. One of the marines assigned to the patrol, a young man who had been in many such firefights, saw my expression and understood what I was feeling. He also understood that the prospect of our having to engage any remaining enemy forces would require all members of the patrol be mentally present, especially the person leading it. He approached me, looked me in the eye and said something that put the night's events into perspective and snapped me back to the present. He said, "Lieutenant, it don't mean nothing; *you've got to let it go.*"

Was he telling me that the casualties we'd suffered didn't matter? Hardly. With words that reflected little sophistication but plenty of wisdom, he was telling me to get over it and get on with it. He'd learned—and he was teaching me—that appropriate and rational grieving relates not only to the gravity of loss, but also to the circumstances in which those losses occur. He was one of my most effective "accountability coaches." By his behavior and his words he helped me understand that accountability is *always* an option, that *the mental choices we make about the setbacks we encounter are ultimately more powerful—have more impact on us—than the setbacks themselves.*

☙

Let me leave you with something that conveys the essence of my thinking and teaching on the subject of accountability. I offer it as a tool for you to use when you catch yourself "bummed out" and looking for alternatives to the mental choices you're using to feed your suffering. I call it "The Rule" and its "Application":

The Rule
Only you can choose the quality of your days.

Application
To have exceptional days,
stop looking for exceptions to **The Rule!**

17. Great Expectations = Great Success
Judy Zerafa

Judy Zerafa is founder of the GO FOR IT! Institute (*www.goforitinstitute.org*), an organization that provides certification for K-12 educators to train them to teach students the how-to's for achieving success. Zerafa also offers corporate as well as private workshops on achieving success (*www.judyzerafa.com*). Her methods address both professional and personal goals. Zerafa's most recent book, *The Simple Easy Diet*, is available online at *www.thesimpleeasydiet.com*.

Since its opening 30 years ago, the XYZ Cleaning Company (not its real name, but the company is real) had shown a profit every quarter until the first quarter of 2009. When the CEO realized he was going to have to tell his 30 managers they would not be getting their routine bonuses, he called me and asked if I would give his management team a pep talk.

I arrived early enough to be able to hear the CFO give the financial report. I understood why the CEO felt his employees needed some good news. As I was introduced and stepped to the podium, I asked the attendees how many of them had been following the financial news over the past 18 months, and how many of them had *expected* their company to experience a profit loss. One by one, every person in the room raised his/her hand, including the CEO. I moved my eyes from face to face and then asked, "If you expected a profit loss, why did you act surprised when you were given the financial report a few minutes ago? I was watching. You all acted surprised."

I told the group I thought they were blessed to have had this experience because I knew if they listened to what I planned to share with them, they would never have to feel this way again.

"What we *expect* in our lives is almost always what we get. You *all* expected to see a loss in profits, and that was exactly what you experienced. The good news is that you can change your expectations."

So much has been written over the past few years about the Law of Attraction. There are many who believe what we "send out" is what we receive. Others are skeptical and lean more toward the idea of luck. Those who are lucky get the breaks; those who are unlucky get the challenges of life.

The universe has immutable laws. One in which we all believe is the law of gravity. I believe the law of attraction is another. It doesn't matter whether you believe in these laws or not. They are precise and always at work.

I think the confusion about the law of attraction is that some of us don't understand what it is that is sent out and then returned in kind. "It" is energy. We create physical energy through our emotions. Every emotion we experience creates a specific vibration. There is, undoubtedly, a more sophisticated and scientific explanation than I am providing here. My interpretation is that our feelings transmit vibrations on a scale or, perhaps more easily visualized, a ladder.

At the top of that ladder are feelings of joy, love and gratitude. You already know how much energy you feel when you are experiencing these emotions. The bottom of the ladder represents the emotions of hopelessness, helplessness and depression. Again, from your own experience, you know that when you are experiencing any of these emotions, you are feeling very little, if any, energy.

The vibrational energy of positive emotions is high. The vibrational energy of negative emotions is low. Without exception, the law of attraction will always return to you whatever is an identical match to the vibration you are transmitting. In other words, when the managers of the XYZ Cleaning Company began reading the news about the current economy and how this country was in for a recession or depression, they started experiencing pessimism and discouragement. The more they listened to the news and economic analysts, the more they talked among each other about how bad things were getting and the further down the ladder of emotions they traveled. By the time I met with them after they had received the news they would not be getting bonuses, most were at the bottom of the ladder feeling hopeless/helpless/depressed.

There are probably many who would argue that in business, it is the overall economy that dictates what is going to happen. I disagree! I think looking at business in that way is just another form of victimhood.

I am president of a nonprofit that trains classroom teachers in the specifics for teaching students *how* to succeed. About 18 months ago, at a monthly board meeting, one of our members began talking about how we had to tighten our belts and get ready for a downturn in funding. I asked the members *not* to do that. I asked if they would do an experiment based on what we stand for and what we teach. I encouraged them to not accept the national, state or local economic gloom and doom as our truth, but to focus on gratitude for the funding we have. I asked everyone to believe that we are unique because what we teach is so critical to our country today. We agreed to think success, talk success and act success.

At our annual board retreat several months later, our non-profit consultant, Richard Male & Associates, began the day by telling our members that in his 31 years of experience, he had never seen a situation where a young nonprofit like us had increased funding by more than 600 percent in an economic climate where every other nonprofit organization was struggling. "You are doing what you teach," he told us. As I looked around the room, it made me proud to know each and every board member had put the best thoughts, words and actions into play. It was a team effort, and in time, students across the country and perhaps around the world will be the recipients of this good energy.

Another dramatic example of expectations is what Bill and Melinda Gates discovered in 2006 and presented in a two-part special on *The Oprah Winfrey Show* regarding the crisis in education in the United States today. "The classroom teacher's *expectations* for his/her students is the single most important factor in how a student performs." Most people who were in the audience those two days were shocked to hear this perspective. But think about it.

What have you *expected* from your family, your friends, your relationship with God, your business? If you are getting what you expect, but not liking what you are getting, you simply need to change your *expectations*. Changing your expectations is a simple thing to do. It is not necessarily easy, but you *can* do it. All expectations are created by thought. To change your expectations, change your thoughts.

If you want your business to succeed, you must expect that it will. Think that it will be successful. Talk about your business successes (with gratitude!). Visualize the success of your business. Thinking success, talking success and visualizing success create powerful emotional energy that activates the law of attraction, delivering what you have called forth. Great Expectations = Great Success. Practice *expecting* what you want ... and you will like what you get.

18. Keep Your Eye on the Doughnut
Ruth Ann Harnisch

Ruth Ann Harnisch is president of the Harnisch Foundation, which has given grants to hundreds of not-for-profit organizations since its founding in 1998. She is a proponent of creative philanthropy whose unusual charitable investments have landed her on *The Oprah Winfrey Show* and the *Today* show. Ruth Ann encourages people to discover the thrill of giving money, time, skills, ideas and other assets to the causes they care about and shares their stories on *www.thrillionaires.org*. Ruth Ann is an International Association of Coaching-certified professional coach. In her *pro bono* practice, Ruth Ann has been a thinking partner to authors, scientists, executives, performers and other dynamic individuals.

Are these good times for your business? In any economic conditions, some businesses thrive. In any circumstances, some people enjoy their work immensely. The essence of good business remains pure and unchanged despite changing conditions.

In my work as a foundation executive and a professional coach, as well as my prior career as a journalist, I've interviewed thousands of people at the pinnacle of their success. What characteristics, behaviors and thought patterns mark the superachievers?

Successful People and Successful Businesses Know What They Stand For

If you happen to work in a nonprofit organization or sit on the board of one, you may have participated in a large group exercise called "the Philanthropy Game." Players are divided into two groups: donors and nonprofits. Each individual creates a personal story. Donors decide how much money they have to invest and what causes they are inclined to support. Nonprofits decide on a mission, a program and a budget. The two groups reunite and the nonprofits try to get the funding they need from the donors, making their cases and competing with all the other good causes for the donors' dollars.

At the end of Round One, the nonprofits who didn't get their funding are out of the game, as are the donors who committed all of their available cash. In Round Two, the nonprofits refine and revise their pitches to compete for a shrinking pool of donor dollars.

As a donor player in that game, I was astonished—and appalled—to see what nonprofit players were willing to do to get money in Round Two. Some nonprofit players offered to create a program tailor-made for a donor player's interests. Some nonprofit players would revamp their missions. In fact, some were willing to completely abandon their original mission if a donor player would give them funding for a different mission! That game taught me, in an exaggerated way, how quickly some people, and some enterprises, will abandon their core principles if their fiscal survival is threatened.

What about you? Are there some principles you will never abandon even if it means you'll go out of business? Are you clear about why you're in business and what principles are at the center of that business? Of course, it's important to be nimble and respond quickly to changing conditions. However, integrity, ethical behavior, moral standards and a guiding light are the unyielding core, the essence.

When we know what we stand for, if we're clear on the principles by which we intend to live, decisions are practically automatic.

Successful People and Successful Businesses Know What Business They're In

Do you have a crystal-clear reason for doing what you're doing? Do you and your team know for sure why the business exists and what the mission is? The essence of your business is its mission. Make the mission central to every decision, and your decisions become easier.

Think of your mission like the destination of a road trip. You know where you want to go, and every decision you make is designed to get you there. You can use a map, read the road signs, consult your GPS, or steer by the stars. You can take the scenic route, the fastest route, the cheapest route, the route with the most roadside rest areas. Every decision, every turn, every stop, can easily be measured against your objective: is this taking us closer to our destination? As you make each decision, keep your mission in mind, and get to the essence: will this choice get us closer to the place we want to go?

Successful People and Successful Businesses Know What They Have

What assets do you have that will help you achieve your goal? It's important to know what's already in your possession to support the accomplishment of your clearly stated purpose.

In my experience as a coach, even the most gifted, talented and successful people underestimate or ignore many of the tools, skills, contacts, qualities, experiences and other assets which could be deployed in the service of their goals. What's in your warehouse, either physical or metaphorical, that can help you hit your mission target?

One of my coaching clients faced an unexpected period of unemployment. Although she was well-qualified and fully engaged in her job search, she was fearful that she might not find work for a long time. She knew that her anxiety was becoming obvious in job interviews, and she did not want to appear desperate.

I asked her to face her fears squarely and say out loud the worst that could happen. She was afraid of being homeless and starving. I asked her how likely that possibility was, and she admitted it was remote. "But suppose it happened?" I asked her. "What if you really did lose your home and did not have money for a meal?"

I invited her to make a list, right then, of every person in her circle of friends and family who would *gladly* offer a place to sleep and food to eat, who would be *happy* to give her a ride or lend her a car, who would press a few dollars into her hand without being asked.

My client surprised herself by coming up with a very long list of people who would be *delighted* to help if she were in need. She calculated that she could have comfortable housing, good food, transportation, emotional support and spiritual comfort for at least a year without being a burden to anyone. "Maybe I should just quit looking for a job!" she joked. Of course, she continued her search, but she brought a new sense of lightness and confidence to the interviews.

Perhaps you are experiencing anxiety or fear about your business situation, and perhaps you, too, could find comfort in taking inventory of the people and things you can count on right now and could turn to in the future. Remember, many people aren't just *willing* to support you in accomplishing your mission; they would be *delighted* to do so. And you probably have a wide variety of assets that you take for granted—until you notice them, appreciate them and use them fully.

Successful People and Successful Businesses Accentuate the Positive

Can you eliminate negative thinking?

The author and expert on thinking, Edward DeBono, created the notion of "thinking hats," encouraging people to assess problems with six different approaches. He believes that only by evaluating situations through different ways of thinking can we come up with the best solution. DeBono's "blue hat" considers the big picture for strategic thinking. The "green hat" looks at the problem creatively. The "red hat" feels the emotional aspects. The "white hat" evaluates the facts without emotion. The "black hat" finds every negative, seeking flaws and obstacles. And the "yellow hat" sees only the positives.

I appreciate DeBono's approach. It's important to consider many points of view, and it's essential to relish the truth with a firm grip on reality. In light of that, it may seem contradictory to cite the advice of an old song: Accentuate the positive, eliminate the negative. After you've considered the facts, even if those facts aren't what you were hoping for, it's still possible to frame statements positively.

As I write this, one of my most beloved clients is in the final hours of his earthly life. He has battled his illness bravely, faced his reality from the diagnosis two years ago, and consistently found a way to view his circumstances in the most positive light possible. He has never shied away from the facts. He has continued to find joy where he could and has helped his family to do the same.

When we first began our work together, he was a healthy young man in the proverbial prime of his life. He was a chief executive who wanted coaching to help him become a better manager. He was a worrier. His language was negative.

I encouraged him to "but out," to eliminate the word "but" from his way of looking at the world. "Substitute the word 'and' for the word 'but,' and you'll be surprised at the difference," I promised. By the time he really needed a positive outlook, he had eliminated much negativity from his attitude and his workplace. He had developed the habit of framing things positively. It was natural for him to say, "I have this health issue *and* I am enjoying my life."

Regardless of your circumstances, you can find a positive way to describe them. And your positive outlook will create more positivity in your own life and in the attitudes of those whose lives you touch. (Hint: negative speech has the same ripple effect, but it's much less enjoyable for everybody!)

Most of my clients have heard me repeat this wise advice, which I learned as a child in Buffalo, New York, where the Mayflower Coffee Shoppe had this sign posted above the door:

> As you ramble on through life, Brother,
> Whatever be your goal,
> Keep your eye upon the doughnut
> And not upon the hole.

There may be no better words to sum up the essence of success in life or in business.

19. The Six Characteristics of Successful People
Tom Hill

Dr. Tom Hill is the owner and president of Eagle Goal Coach. He is a noted coach, author and speaker, delivering more than 75 presentations a year. Tom is the author of *Living at the Summit* and the co-author of *Life Plan for Living at the Summit* and *Chicken Soup for the Entrepreneur's Soul*. Prior to founding Eagle Goal Coach, he was the owner, president and CEO of RE/MAX Dixie Region as well as a university administrator.

In 1986, after 26 years in public education, including 14 years at the university level, I left to pursue an entrepreneurial career. I started with a partner owning the rights to RE/MAX of Kentucky/Tennessee, Southern Ohio, Alabama, Mississippi and Louisiana. Then in 1990 I purchased 100 percent of the three southern states known as the RE/MAX Dixie Region. In the beginning we had four franchisees and 40 sales associates.

In 1993 I added a 25 percent partner and together we grew the business to 100 offices and 1,000 sales associates. In 1994 I became fascinated with why some of our franchisees were very successful, while others were less so. I wondered, were successful folks just lucky, in the right place at the right time, or did they have some key common characteristics that set them apart from those who were not as successful? In 1996 I became involved in putting together our book, *Chicken Soup for the Entrepreneur's Soul*. This opened doors to study successful individuals. As time passed, folks I considered to be already successful started coming to me and asking me if I would be their "coach." Coaching others for success became my passion, my avocation.

My personal success journey began in 1984 when my wife, Betty, and I were introduced to motivational speaker and author Jim Rohn. Jim taught us the importance of prioritizing our core values—identifying the important things in our lives.

We decided that summer that our priorities were, in this order, spiritual health, physical health, relationships, emotional health, intellectual development and financial prosperity. Little did I realize at the time how important this experience was in moving us forward in our journey towards success. Your priorities may, of course, be different than ours, but my advice is to know what yours are and stay true to those core values. Once you've clarified your core values, rank each one on a scale of one to 10 and then decide which one or ones you will focus on.

Once I started designing my life around these values, I discovered that when you focus on becoming the best person you can in the five value categories of spiritual health, physical health, relationships, emotional health and intellectual development, you will attract the success you've been trying to achieve in the sixth value category, financial prosperity. You see, money is attracted, not pursued.

All of this led me to define what I consider to be the six characteristics of successful people.

1. Personal development. Successful individuals are committed to personal development—committed to becoming the very best person they can be in the five value categories of spiritual health, physical health, relationships, emotional health and intellectual development.

2. One person can change your life forever. Successful individuals are disciplined networkers. They either consciously or subconsciously create a powerful network. Because of who they have become in these five key value areas, they attract other successful people.

3. One idea, well executed, can change your life forever. Jack Canfield and Mark Victor Hansen (creators of the *Chicken Soup for the Soul* book series) had a very simple idea: gather great stories, write them down and sell millions of books. It worked. Turn off the TV; read a book a week; listen to educational CDs; have a thirst for knowledge; birth a new idea.

4. Be a lifelong learner. Study principles of success. There are literally hundreds of success principles; it's your task to determine the ones that work best for you. If I had to pick only one "success" book, it would be Felix Dennis' *How to Get Rich*. His eight principles are priceless—I still have them on my bedroom mirror.

5. Discipline. If I had to pick one characteristic that is most important it would be discipline. If you don't have discipline, the odds are against you. Some say that you can change a habit in 21 days. I don't believe this. In my experience, it takes about 18 months to completely erase an old habit and truly create a new one. It takes discipline, daily discipline. If in sales you need to make 40 cold calls a day and if you only make 20, you will fail. If you are overweight, discipline in your diet and exercise will make a difference.

6. Odds in my favor. Whatever I'm doing, I want to stack the odds in my favor. If I'm riding a motorcycle, I always wear a helmet. It puts the odds in my favor. When I climb the Colorado Fourteeners (the 54 peaks of the Colorado Rockies that rise over 14,000 feet), I start and finish before noon—before the lighting storms come. This puts the odds in my favor. Live debt-free. This puts the financial odds in your favor.

I went from a low-paid educator to a millionaire entrepreneur in three years using the principles and values I've described. Anyone with average intelligence and the desire can accomplish amazing things. Most folks do not dream big enough; most people are severely self-limiting. Once I understood the principles of success, my life was like a rocket ship, literally taking me places I'd never dreamed of because I'd been too self-limiting; that is, until I found what I believe are the key principles. I realize not everyone will agree with me, and that's fine; however, I've witnessed not only in my own life, but in the lives of others, how these principles can create what Joseph Jaworski calls "predictable miracles." I challenge you to make the choices that enable you to live a life of predictable miracles.

20. CRAVE Your Goals!

Tricia Molloy

Tricia Molloy loves to remind people how wise they are! She's a professional speaker, business consultant and author of *Divine Wisdom at Work: 10 Universal Principles for Enlightened Entrepreneurs* and the upcoming book, *Take Your Higher Self to Work: 5 Best Practices for Success.* More information can be found at *www.triciamolloy.com* or by e-mail at *tricia@triciamolloy.com.*

Even though it was in the early '90s, I remember my initial experience with Unity as if it were yesterday. Like many who attend a Unity service for the first time, I had this overwhelming knowing that I was home and then I cried. It took several weeks of services before I didn't cry any more at Unity North Atlanta Church—the feeling of "being home" has never diminished.

Since I am a marketing consultant—I've had my own PR business since 1988—I volunteered to help spread the word about this empowering spiritual community. Then I served on the church's board of directors for seven years. It was my board experience that inspired me to write a book about how to capitalize on the power of spiritual principles in the workplace. It's called *Divine Wisdom at Work: 10 Universal Principles for Enlightened Entrepreneurs.*

I had always used principles like affirmations, visualization and gratitude in my life and my work. Through Unity, I discovered the laws behind these principles and connected with others who also embraced them. Once my book came out in 2006, I launched my speaking and training business, Working With Wisdom. I began presenting talks, workshops and retreat programs for companies and business associations. This work divinely expressed my life purpose: *Through support and by example, I inspire others to follow their dreams and live joyfully on purpose.*

When I launched my speaking and training business, I often covered all 10 universal principles. Though my audiences seemed inspired, I could tell they were often overwhelmed. Much of this information was new to them, and it was a challenge to figure out how to start putting what they learned into practice. So I tapped into my own wisdom, took the five most practical and accessible principles and came up with a juicy acronym that would be easy to remember and share. "CRAVE Your Goals!® Five Steps to Attract What You Desire and Deserve" has become my most popular program. I've shared it with such organizations as Home Depot, UPS, AT&T, Delta Air Lines and the National Association of Women Business Owners. I'd like to share it with you.

We all have professional and personal goals that we're trying to achieve. It may be getting that promotion or new job, attracting ideal clients and customers, losing 20 pounds or becoming debt-free. And then there are those bodacious, big-dream goals like owning a vacation home, traveling throughout Europe or establishing a foundation to support worthy causes. When we truly commit to our goals and crave them with our heart and soul, we engage the energy of the universe and receive what we need to make our dreams come true. Commit to follow these five CRAVE steps to attract what you desire and deserve.

1) Clean Out the Clutter

Clutter distracts and confuses us and drains our energy. It often keeps us from doing what's most important and gets in the way of our goals. If your office tends to be messy, imagine you finally get inspired to really clean out the clutter. You throw away the garbage and clean up your desktop. You organize your files and, if you are fortunate enough to choose your own clients, take the files of inactive clients and put them into two piles—the ones you want to work with again and the ones you hope you never ever see, not even in the supermarket. You clean up and organize the first pile of files, put them back in the cabinet and call a few of these inactive clients to inquire if you can work with them again or request referrals to others like them. As for that other pile of files, throw it out. For some, this is too bold a move. At the least, box them up and store them somewhere else. You'll immediately feel the energy lighten up in your workspace.

Once you've cleaned out your office clutter, you'll notice the phone begins to ring, new business and ideas spring up, and projects that were put on hold get back on track. That's because you have inadvertently activated a universal law: "The universe abhors a vacuum." So when you clean out the physical clutter, you create the space for the universe to fill it with what serves your highest good.

In addition to physical clutter, it's also emotional clutter—the regrets and resentments—and the technical clutter—information overload and an unhealthy dependence on the Internet and your cell phone. Commit to identifying clutter in your life and start to clean it out. You will be rewarded with more clarity and energy as you CRAVE your goals.

2) Raise Your Vibrations

This universal law states: Energy attracts like energy. We are all energy beings and we all vibrate at different levels at different times. *Vibration* is just another word for feelings and emotions. When we vibrate at a high level, this energy is governed by love and trust and peace and is positive and constructive. We will attract people and circumstances that vibrate at that same level. Conversely, when we are consumed by fear and worry, when we are stressed out and burned out and feel unappreciated, we will vibrate at a low, negative, destructive level, and we will attract people and circumstances that vibrate at that same level.

To increase and maintain a high vibration, commit to love and nurture yourself. Eat healthy, exercise, enjoy a hobby, play, sing, laugh, forgive, limit your time watching TV news, seek out positive people, give thanks, spend time in nature, smile more often, and practice random and not-so-random acts of kindness.

My teenage daughter, Allyson, and I were at a drive-through restaurant one afternoon. As I was paying my bill, I decided to pay for the woman in the car behind me. The only thing the woman saw as we drove away was my license plate: URDVINE. We were giddy wondering what she thought when she was told her bill had been paid and what she may have told her family that evening. For $5.65, that random act of kindness raised our vibrations and probably raised hers too. We suspect she may have also paid it forward and treated someone else to a random act of kindness.

Commit to make your own list and schedule these activities into your day until they become habits. Form a "high vibration" club with your co-workers and friends so you can have fun supporting each other.

3) Affirm Success

Affirmations are powerful statements to remind us what we know to be true, despite what others may say or what our ego may say when it plants that seed of doubt. The most effective affirmations are short, positive and in the present.

Here are a few examples. If you want to be chosen for a supervisory position, your affirmation should include the qualities you possess that would serve you in that role. You might affirm: "I am a dynamic, empowering leader." If you tend to wake up each morning wondering how you'll ever get through your burgeoning to-do list, you might affirm: "I have more than enough time and energy to accomplish the most important goals today." If you are struggling with direction and finding the right resources to get the job done, you might affirm: "I am open to receive guidance and support." Commit to write down your affirmations and post them prominently—on your bathroom mirror, on the dashboard of your car and at your desk. Say them out loud throughout the day and share them with others.

4) Visualize

Every top athlete has harnessed the power of visualization. The runner sees herself breaking through the tape at the end of the race, and the golfer sees the hole-in-one. What can you visualize about your goals? Perhaps it's making a persuasive presentation that motivates your audience to take action. Or you might visualize working in a clean, organized office. It takes more than just seeing to get the results. Visualization is a three-step, repetitive process. To give it the power you need to succeed, engage all your senses. What do you hear, smell, touch and taste? Then, infuse your vision with the positive emotions you would feel if this were a reality—like happiness, pride and maybe even relief. Commit to seeing your goals as "real" and they soon will be.

One of the best ways to activate the power of visualization is to use a treasure map or vision board. It's simply a bulletin board placed somewhere you can see it every day. You adorn it with things that reflect what you want to manifest. Use pictures and words clipped from magazines and newspapers, kind notes from clients or colleagues, and your own photos and postcards. You get the idea. Fill your map and your mind with the images and messages of what you want your life and work to look like. Remember to tend to it regularly. Prune the pieces that no longer resonate and add others. It's a colorful, organic reflection of your best self.

5) Express Thanks

What you focus on expands. What you appreciate appreciates. It's a universal law. That's why it's so important to cultivate an attitude of gratitude. Commit to write in a gratitude journal a few nights a week, listing all the things you're thankful for at work—a great boss, doing what you love—and adding at least one unique entry each time—"I spoke with everyone I called today" or "I completed that major project ahead of schedule." This programs you to become more aware of what's going right.

Use gratitude to transform challenging relationships. For one week, focus on what you appreciate about that person and refrain from criticism. As it relates to your professional, personal and bodacious, big-dream goals, give thanks for what is and what will be in anticipation of your accomplishments.

By committing to CRAVE your goals, you will enhance your journey and accelerate your success.

Section V

New Skills for a New Millennium

21. Say "Yes" to What Really Matters in Your Life

Martha Lynn

Martha Lynn, Ph.D., has held executive positions in a variety of industries, including financial institutions, a national engineering and architectural firm, and a regional health-care system. Martha was a partner in HCAP International, a consulting business, before joining Unity. As the vice president of SpiritPath at Unity Village, her responsibilities include oversight of Unity's hotel and conference center, retreats, events and workshops, weddings and meeting planning, the Unity Bookstore and Coffee Shop and Unity Inn.

Charlotte and I have the great privilege of interviewing wonderfully accomplished businesspeople every week on our *Good Business* radio program. With this book, you now have the privilege of reading about their insights, wisdom and recommendations for leading and working inside principle-based organizations.

All of our remarkable guests have shown us ways to lead with integrity, grace and clarity, regardless of our titles. One of the questions Charlotte and I always ask our radio guests is, "What is your best advice for how each of our listeners can create a more meaningful life?"

Without exception, the answers revolve around the fact that we are all responsible and accountable for the choices we make. Our guests may not always use those exact words, but inevitably their messages hit at the heart of what each of us controls—ourselves.

One of my favorite Bible verses is "Choose this day whom you will serve" (Joshua 24:15). I am responsible and accountable for my choices—every moment of every day. Do I choose discernment over judgment, abundance over lack, possibility over problem, health over dis-ease, peace over anxiety, openness over being opinionated, joy over despair, love over fear? If not, why not?

The way we choose to think, feel and act directly comes from one of two places—our egos or our higher self. If ego or personality is at the root of our thinking, feeling and acting, our decisions/choices may be based on lack, survival or fear. None of these would come from our higher self. Rather, our higher self shows up as possibility thinking, gratitude and inquisitiveness.

When we listen to our higher self, choices, decisions, thoughts, feelings and actions take on a whole new realm of possibility. Our perceptions are more objective, our thoughts are more compassionate, our feelings are more loving and our actions are in integrity. This is territory that is not just relevant to CEOs or executive teams, but to every individual who shows up each day and contributes to the success of their organization. Martin Luther King Jr. wrote "If you are called to be a street sweeper, sweep streets even as Michelangelo painted, or Beethoven composed music, or Shakespeare wrote poetry. Sweep streets so well that all the hosts of heaven and earth will pause to say, "Here lived a great street sweeper who did his job well."[1]

Dr. King's quote is one that is steeped in *choice, intention* and *right action* and that power is ever-present with each breath we take. Isn't choice something we would all say yes to each and every moment? Of course, and yet we often unconsciously say no to choice because we rely on that automatic pilot—our habits, our ego-self—that we have relied on for many years. We don't even think about it. Many of us manage hourly, daily, weekly and yearly with our habits and ego guiding our thoughts, feelings and actions. To be unconscious to our own light and power could be due to many things: our lack of awareness of who we really are, our lack of discipline, our lack of a plan, our willingness to play small. As Marianne Williamson most eloquently states:

> Our deepest fear is not that we are inadequate.
> Our deepest fear is that we are powerful beyond measure ...
> You are a child of God. Your playing small does not serve the World ...
> We were born to make manifest the glory of God that is within us ...[2]

This quote offers us an opportunity to reflect on our willingness to seek another way of being in our lives and in our work ... or not.

The choice is always within us, and so my message is addressed to those of you who are willing to choose to be in the world differently. To look at work as a laboratory in which the ego takes a lesser role, and the light of your being takes center stage. I continue to be a student each and every day of what I'm about to share with you. The old saw "we teach what we need to learn" should be in bold letters on my office door. So as I speak to you through this writing, please know I am a student with you.

My contribution to our book focuses on three simple spiritual practices that can be used no matter what position you hold in an organization. We don't have to hold a management or executive title to lead and show up in ways that move the organization forward toward its mission and vision. We just need to clearly remember and recognize who we are at the core of our being and act from that place of love and strength.

The good news is that these spiritual practices for changing our way of being in the work world are simple. The bad news is, they are not easy. Old habits don't always die easily. The ego can be a fierce resistor. It does not like change. However, all of us can and do change as we master these three powerful spiritual tools: intention, self-observation and authentic action. Here's the process:

1. Identify your intention. One of our *Good Business* guests, Maria Nemeth, author of *Mastering Life's Energies* and owner of the Academy of Coaching Excellence, trains coaches and shares her work through classes and writing. Maria teaches her students to start each day by asking: "Who am I willing to *be* in order to produce an extraordinary result out of this day?"

What better way than to start each day with an intention of how we want to show up. The beauty of intentions is that we can bring them into awareness in a moment's reflection. It's great to start each day with intentions, but it is also useful to pause and set them for each meeting, customer service opportunity or difficult conversation. Just think of all of the opportunities we have during our workday to clearly focus on how we intend to show up in the moment.

Charlotte and I set a prayer intention before each of our radio interviews, which is to be focused and clear in our questions and to listen with love and compassion. This intention creates an energy field of respect and openness to possibility. We never know what will be brought forth from our guests or from each of us, but we do rest in the knowing that our listeners are blessed by the information that comes from our time together.

Unconscious intentions are set all the time. Our responsibility is to set intentions consciously from our deep core of knowing, the spark of divinity that resides in us all. Only then are we playing at the top of our game with unlimited ability to contribute. This universal law of mind action never fails us—whatever we focus on becomes our reality.

2. Become a self-observer. We have to be able to observe our thoughts and the stories we are telling ourselves about our encounters. I am a great storyteller and meaning-making machine. I can listen to a few words in a team meeting, phone call or dialogue with another and create an entire three-act play. Ego loves drama, fear and power, and many of my stories are great tragedies.

It's important for me to quickly observe the stories and stresses I am experiencing in that moment and to be able to redirect my reactions in ways that will be helpful to me and others. I've been privileged to experience HeartMath® as both a consultant and trainer and several years ago I brought that training into the health-care organization in which I worked. We conducted a controlled study with highly educated and trained health-care professionals that showed the positive impact of using HeartMath tools to reduce stress. There was a significant decrease in stress in a number of variables in the experimental group (those who practiced HeartMath techniques) compared to the control group. The Freeze-Frame technique (© HeartMath LLC) is one self-observation technique that has been scientifically proven over the years to have significant impact on one's health and well-being. You can find out more about these great tools and research by going to *www.heartmath.org.*

Being a self-observer means you have the ability to monitor your thoughts and feelings to be sure they are coming from an open, loving and sacred place so that, when we speak, make decisions or take action, we know that this comes from our highest power rather than from habitual thinking, feeling and acting.

The easy part is that we always have the capacity to self-observe; the hard part is remembering to do it. Once we remember, we can shift instantly from ego to our higher presence and make another choice (intention). Introverts and extroverts alike can easily maneuver through opportunities for intention and self-observation. My introverted self likes to take five deep breaths before I speak or as I'm listening. That is my cue to self-observe and reconnect with my true intentions and higher power. However, I have observed my extroverted friends shifting in the moment and formulating their language to align with their intentions. Self-observation does not require any skill other than to pause, reflect and ask: "Am I thinking, feeling and preparing to act in a way that is in alignment with my higher self intention?"

3. Take authentic action. "Authentic" in this context means to act from our higher source—our intention—not from the ego, but from that spark of divinity that is in all of us. When we act from that place, we know we are being true to ourselves. We are expressing energy that is coming from our soul. We are spirit in action.

When we act from this powerful authentic place, we may not always get what we want, but we know that we have been true to ourselves; we have acted in integrity. We have brought to the table an energy that is empowering and enabling. We have demonstrated a new way to lead, whether we are the executive or an individual contributor. The beautiful thing about taking authentic action is that the energy shifts whether we are in a meeting or sitting at our desk facing a critical decision.

It's a beautiful thing to see and experience the shifting of energy in a room. That shift occurs because an individual has chosen to be responsible for making a wiser choice through self-observation, setting a different intention and acting on that decision. When this is done, people contribute differently, safety is restored, and possibility and potential have a forum for expression.

The key is courage. Do we have the courage to set intentions that come from a place of love rather than one of lack and self-preservation? Do we have the courage to self-observe and take responsibility and be accountable for our thoughts, feelings and actions? Do we have the courage to shift from habits that we have relied on for decades—our frame of reference for how the world works? And do we have the courage to act from the Christ presence that is in all of us—our spark of divinity—a place of love? As Kahlil Gibran says so beautifully in *The Prophet*:

And what is it to work with love?

It is to weave the cloth with threads drawn from your heart, even as if your beloved were to wear that cloth.

It is to build a house with affection, even as if your beloved were to dwell in that house ...

Work is love made visible.[3]

And so it is my pleasure to remind myself and all of you what we already know: Choice is the only freedom we really have. As we go about our work, whatever form that might take, let's all remember to say yes to what really matters in our life; to say yes to choice; to take time to pause, reflect and choose our intentions carefully; to self-observe our thoughts and feelings; and to act authentically from that sacred place of love and strength.

May all of our work be love made visible.

22. Quantum Skills for a New Millennium
Charlotte Shelton

Charlotte Shelton, Ed.D., is president/CEO of Unity, an international transdenominational organization dedicated to helping people apply positive spiritual principles in their daily lives. She was previously chair of the Management and Marketing Division at Rockhurst University, Kansas City, Missouri, and president of WiseWork Coaching and Consulting. She is the author of *Quantum Leaps: 7 Skills for Workplace ReCreation* and co-author of *The NeXt Revolution: What Gen X Women Want at Work and How Their Boomer Bosses Can Help Them Get It.*

The world made a quantum leap in the 20th century. Many of the mind-boggling changes were a result of technology; and many of these technological breakthroughs were made possible by a new theory of physics called *quantum mechanics*. This term was introduced in the 1920s to describe the physics of the subatomic realm. The subatomic realm refers to everything in the physical world that is smaller than an atom. Computers, the Internet, bar code readers and laser surgery represent only a few of the innovative inventions birthed as a result of this new theory.

In fact, it would be quite accurate to say that quantum physics has ushered in a new *quantum age*. It has revolutionized the way we live our lives and do our work; yet this new theory has had almost no impact on how most Westerners "think." Very few of us have updated our mental paradigms to align with the new science. Thus, we find ourselves working in organizations that are changing at warp speed—without the new skills that are prerequisite for gracefully thriving in such a change-filled environment.

This article introduces a new quantum skill set that can enable us to thrive in an era of exponential change. These quantum skills are ancient and futuristic, scientific and spiritual, simple and difficult. They are key skills for riding the rapids of 21st-century organizational change, though they originated in the mystical wisdom of ages past. Many ancient spiritual teachings, as well as many current state-of-the-art psychological theories, are based on concepts that are similar to the quantum principles from which these seven skills are derived.

The skills are: (1) *Quantum Seeing*, the ability to *see* intentionally; (2) *Quantum Thinking*, the ability to *think* paradoxically; (3) *Quantum Feeling*, the ability to *feel* vitally alive; (4) *Quantum Knowing*, the ability to *know* intuitively; (5) *Quantum Acting*, the ability to *act* responsibly; (6) *Quantum Trusting*, the ability to *trust* life's process; and (7) *Quantum Being*, the ability to *be* in relationship. The Quantum Skills Model shown below reflects the interrelationships among these seven skills.

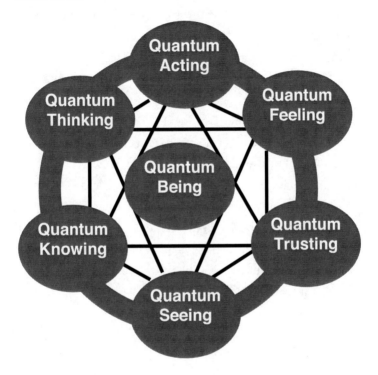

The Quantum Skills Model

The three skills connected to the inverted triangle—quantum seeing, quantum thinking and quantum feeling—are psychological in nature. They are based on three basic psychological principles: (1) Human perception is highly subjective (quantum seeing); (2) Creative thinking requires the development of the right hemisphere of the brain (quantum thinking); and (3) Human feelings are not caused by external events but by our internal self-talk (quantum feeling). Understanding these basic psychological constructs enables us to live and work more intentionally, more creatively and more responsibly; however, these three skills alone do not necessarily provide a deep sense of meaning and purpose.

In order to bring more Spirit into our lives and workplaces, additional skills are needed—skills that shift the focus from "me" to "we," from egocentric self-interest to concern for the good of the whole. The next three quantum skills are grounded in three universal spiritual principles: (1) We live in an intelligent universe (quantum knowing); (2) Everything in the universe is interrelated (quantum acting); and (3) The universe uses chaos to create order (quantum trusting). The three *spiritual* skills are shown on the model's upright triangle. The seventh skill, quantum being, is intricately connected to each of the other quantum skills. Its central position in the model reflects this connection.

The Psychological Skills

Quantum Seeing

The first skill, quantum seeing, is based on the quantum discovery that the world we live in is not nearly as objective as most of us believe. Both quantum theory and research in human perception suggest that over 80 percent of what is seen in the external world is a function of internal assumptions and beliefs. Yet most of us work in organizations that have little regard for the subjectivity of external reality. Reality, or at least the individual experience thereof, is

directly related to those things that individuals think about.
Author Gary Zukav explains:

> Reality is what we take to be true. What we take to be
> true is what we believe. What we believe is based upon
> our perceptions. What we perceive depends upon what
> we look for. What we look for depends on what we
> think. What we think depends on what we perceive.
> What we perceive determines what we believe. What
> we believe determines what we take to be true. What
> we take to be true is our reality.[1]

Our beliefs reinforce our perceptions, and our perceptions
reinforce our beliefs; unfortunately, it is not easy to break this
cycle. It is learned early and controlled primarily at an unconscious level of awareness. However, we can learn to become
more aware of our intentions, and, as we learn to change our
intentions, our perceptions shift accordingly. Psychologist and
author Mihaly Csikszentmihalyi believes that intention is the
psychological process by which reality is constructed.[2]
Intentions cause us to pay attention to certain stimuli while
totally ignoring a plethora of other perceptual possibilities.
What we pay attention to becomes our reality. The skill of quantum seeing reminds us to consciously select our intentions.

For example, if a manager sets a clear intention to improve
inventory costs, he/she will begin to notice (attend to) information that normally would not have been perceived. The
manager may begin to discuss the matter with other individuals in the firm, seeking out suggestions for improvement.
He/she may consult with suppliers as to how they can assist
with the matter. Production runs may be carefully reviewed

for possible improvement. Just-in-time inventory techniques may be studied and considered for implementation. An inventory consultant might be hired to provide advice. The manager may visit other businesses to search out new ideas. Professional publications could be reviewed for new techniques and procedures. Transportation networks and services may be more carefully analyzed. All of these actions were, of course, already available to the manager; however, they were perceptually ignored until a conscious intention was made that shifted attention. Clear intention serves as a magnifying glass. It provides a new lens through which managers can make new perceptual choices—choices that otherwise would have been missed.

Organizations would function quite differently if everyone—managers and individual contributors—were able to create intentionally, fully conscious of the role that intention plays in all that is seen and experienced. Well-known techniques like affirmations, dream boards or treasure maps can serve as intention reminders. As we use these verbal and visual aids, we become increasingly conscious of our desires and our attention spontaneously shifts. The skill of quantum seeing enables us to live life intentionally!

Quantum Thinking

The second skill, quantum thinking, is derived from quantum physics research that suggests that the physical universe functions in seemingly illogical and paradoxical ways. The most obvious quantum paradox is that the three-dimensional material world is composed solely of invisible energy. Furthermore, this energy often makes sudden, totally unpredictable quantum leaps, tunneling through barriers in ways that are both illogical and impossible at the macro level of reality. Quantum tunneling is totally illogical; yet it is the basis of the Josephson junction, a key process in superconductivity. Josephson junctions operate as extremely fast switching devices. They are a key design feature in a highly sensitive measuring instrument called a SQUID (superconducting quantum interference device). Because of the highly illogical quantum tunneling effect, physicians can now identify and treat minute abnormalities within the human brain. Illogical processes can result in highly practical applications.

Unfortunately, many organizations still rely primarily on logical, linear, black-and-white thinking skills. Eleanor Rosch, a psychology professor at the University of California, Berkeley, demonstrated that the obsession with binary thinking originates in the structure of the brain.[3] Over the centuries, the human brain has added layers, evolving from the early reptilian to the limbic, to the much more recent neocortex (outer layer of the brain). The two lower brain centers are actually incapable of conceptualizing multiple options. So even though the neocortex can create and choose among unlimited options, much of the time we still operate out of lower brain centers, categorizing and organizing information with minimal cognitive effort. Our logical, linear educational systems and either/or organizational decision-making processes reinforce this neurological propensity. Consequently, most adults generally demonstrate less than 10 percent of the creativity of a typical child.

If organizations are to think and act "outside the box," it is apparent that logical, rational, binary thought processes are inadequate. Many 21st-century organizational challenges are paradoxical, posing questions that cannot be answered by rational, binary thinking. For example, how can managers balance their responsibility to stockholders with responsibility to employees, customers and the environment? How can short-term operating goals be achieved while maintaining a long-term focus? Or how can we decrease errors while also improving speed? The ability to think paradoxically will no doubt be a key to creating highly innovative solutions to these questions and myriad other 21st-century organizational challenges.

In order to think paradoxically, we must awaken the capacities of the right hemisphere of the brain—the side of the brain that thinks in images, not words, and is therefore not bound by verbal language and logic. The right brain can gather up seemingly unrelated ideas and arrange them into highly creative idea constellations, thereby bypassing the left brain's propensity for binary thinking. The right brain has another important creative advantage. It can process millions of visual images in microseconds and solve problems exponentially faster than the clock-bound left hemisphere. Each time we choose to visualize versus think in words, we literally disconnect from the linear passage of time. Thus, through the process of imagistic thinking, we can escape the tyranny of time and enter a realm where seemingly opposite options can effortlessly synthesize into highly creative solutions. The skill of quantum thinking provides an ongoing stream of highly innovative, often illogical, yet pragmatic solutions. In order for our 21st-century organizations to thrive, and perhaps even survive, this skill must be developed.

Quantum Feeling

The third skill, quantum feeling, is based on the premise that humans are composed of the same energy as the rest of the universe and are, therefore, subject to universal laws of energy excitation. Recent research at the Institute of HeartMath suggests that the human heart is a primary source of power for the mind-body system.[4] The heart generates the strongest electromagnetic signal in the human body, and the power of that signal is primarily a function of thoughts and emotions. Negative emotions (e.g., frustration, fear, anger, conflict and stress) decrease coherence in the heart's electromagnetic waves, causing the mind-body system to lose energy. Positive emotions (e.g., love, caring, compassion and appreciation) increase coherence, thus increasing energy.

This research confirms what many of us already know intuitively. Negative emotions exhaust and positive emotions energize. Knowing this to be true does not, however, solve the epidemic of stress, conflict and burnout in today's organizations. Fast-paced schedules drain energy. Stress-filled jobs exhaust employees. Interpersonal differences create conflict. We all desire health and vitality; but too often we experience tiredness and dis-ease. The skill of quantum feeling enables us to feel good internally regardless of what happens externally. As we use this skill, we learn how to change the chemistry of our bodies by changing the feelings of our hearts. We become increasingly aware of the perceptual choice point between an external stimulus and a subsequent internal response, and we begin to recognize that our energy is never depleted by other people or events, but rather by our perceptual choices.

The Institute of HeartMath research also suggests that we can maintain higher levels of energy and vitality simply by choosing to focus on the positive aspects of our experiences.[5] Seeing "negative" events from a positive perspective does require one to think paradoxically. If we suddenly find ourselves unemployed, it is only logical to catastrophize. However, if we do so, we will see only those perceptual clues that support our negative thinking. We may notice our bills accumulating. We'll likely see "bad" news about the economy everywhere we turn. On the other hand, if we can view the situation in an atypical way, seeing it with appreciation, we can begin to see the hidden opportunities. As we focus on the positive aspects, our heart's electromagnetic waves become coherent and the brain's waves spontaneously follow (physicists call this *entrainment*). From this more coherent state of mind, we see opportunities that we would have missed had we remained in a state of negativity. The opportunities would have been there all along; but our emotionally induced cognitive incoherence simply would have made us perceptually blind.

The skill of quantum feeling has enormous impact on issues such as motivation, burnout, stress and job satisfaction. Organizational life will change significantly when enough of us can release our dependence on external rewards and take full personal responsibility for bringing purpose, passion and vitality to our jobs by choosing appreciation rather than frustration, faith rather than fear, and accountability rather than victimization. I can't wait!

The Spiritual Skills

Quantum Knowing

The fourth skill, quantum knowing, is derived from quantum field theory. Energy fields are, in the language of physics, the ground state of all that is. Einstein once commented that "fields are the only reality."[6] The universe is not filled with energy fields; rather, the universe emerges out of an underlying quantum field. This underlying sea of potential appears to be infinite, omnipresent and omnipotent. It is both indescribable and incalculable. The quantum field is believed to contain Bose-Einstein condensates, which are the most highly ordered and highly unified structures yet found in the universe. Danah Zohar is one of a growing number of physicists who believe that Bose-Einstein processes in the brain may create the neurological structures that are prerequisite to human consciousness.[7] If subsequent research validates a relationship between Bose-Einstein condensates and consciousness, it will lend support to the hypothesis that the quantum field itself is conscious. Consciousness, therefore, may not be a function of evolutionary sophistication, but instead may be the primary substance of physical reality. Harvard biologist George Wald explains:

> Mind, rather than emerging as a late outgrowth in the evolution of life, has existed always as the matrix, the

source and condition of physical reality ... the stuff of which physical reality is composed is mind-stuff. It is mind that has composed a physical universe that breeds life, and so eventually evolves creatures that know and create.[8]

The universe is basically a set of signals or a field of information. It is much more like a "great thought" than the "great-machine" metaphor of the Newtonian paradigm. Quantum knowing is the ability to know intuitively—to connect in nonsensory ways with information in this quantum field of potentiality. Author/speaker Jean Houston, using the metaphor of superconductivity, explains how meditation affects our intuitive ability:

> In most electrical flow systems there is a resistance, analogous to a turned-on light bulb impeding the flow of current, which creates the practical uses for the electrical current. But in superconductive states the electrons can flow unimpeded in perpetual motion through a flow loop. This may be what is happening in the experience of deep meditation: neurons become superconductive flow systems, phase-coherent with other neurons by virtue of quantum tunneling. Resistance is overcome, the usual kinds of perceptual and psychological lenses are no longer operative, and the brain becomes a very different instrument, one that is available to receive messages from the primary reality.[9]

In this superconductive state, our ability to access previously unknown information increases appreciably. We discover a capacity for wisdom that may be infinite. We become one with the quantum field—the cosmic database of infinite intelligence which some call God.

Harvard University psychology professor Ellen Langer has developed a theory of mindful decision-making.[10] Her research suggests that gathering information does not necessarily lead to better decisions. In fact, organizations typically focus on an impossible goal—reducing uncertainty through data collection. This is futile because even the amount of information that could be gathered about the simplest of decisions, such as developing a new product or selecting a supplier, can involve limitless research. Rather than focusing on gathering information, Langer's theory focuses on staying aware (mindfulness). She points out that a belief in *certainty* is actually a huge disadvantage. Certainty leads to mindlessness. When one is certain, he/she typically ceases to pay attention. On the other hand, uncertainty keeps us attentive both to the external conditions and to our internal intuitions. Mindfulness keeps us connected to the quantum field of infinite information.

As we begin to incorporate mindfulness into our daily work routines, we will create whole-brain organizations that honor both sides of the brain, valuing intuitive knowing as much as rational analysis. Someday we will look back at concepts such as empowerment or open-book management with amusement. After all, how can one person empower another if everyone has access to the same cosmic database? As more and more of us learn to use the skill of quantum knowing, we will help create authentic learning organizations—

organizations in which all the stakeholders deeply value learning from the inside out.

Quantum Acting

The fifth skill, quantum acting, is premised on the quantum concept of nonseparability and its by-product, non-local causation. At the subatomic level, two systems once connected remain connected, even across great distances of time and space. Any measurement of one of these systems affects the second system instantaneously. These complex "from a distance" interactions are explained by a uniquely quantum principle, the principle of nonseparability, which violates the most basic principle of relativity, that nothing can travel faster than the speed of light.

Even though Einstein never accepted the principle of non-separability, today this principle is a fundamental concept in quantum theory. Its technological applications will soon create quantum computers in which all the components respond instantaneously to a change in the state of one component. The potential capacity of quantum computers is truly amazing. They will be capable of performing all possible computations simultaneously (quantum parallelism). Strings of hydrogen atoms rather than arrays of transistors will hold bits of information. Atomic encoding will enable a quantum computer to simulate the behavior of any quantum system using quantum processes such as superimposition and non-local correlation. According to a *Scientific American* article, "A 40-bit quantum computer could recreate in little more than, say, 100 steps, a quantum system that would take a classical computer, having a trillion bits, years to simulate."[11]

Action at a distance (nonlocal causation) is about to transform life as it is presently known through astounding technological advances; but more important, this same principle has the potential to shift our view of ourselves and our relationship to others and to the physical universe. British science writer John Gribbin explains:

> They [research studies] tell us that particles that were once together in an interaction remain in some sense parts of a single system, which responds together to further interactions. Virtually everything we see and touch and feel is made up of collections of particles that have been involved in interactions with others right back through time, to the Big Bang in which the universe as we know it came into being. The atoms in my body are made of particles that once jostled in close proximity in the cosmic fireball with particles that are now part of a distant star, and particles that form the body of some living creature on some distant, undiscovered planet. Indeed, the particles that make up my body once jostled in close proximity and interacted with the particles that make up your body.[12]

Everything in the universe is a part of a correlated, complex whole in which each part influences and is influenced by every other part. Quantum acting is the ability to act with concern for the whole—the whole self, the whole organization, the whole society and the whole planet. This skill can be used to design lives of impeccable action—lives that focus on intentions that are good for both self and for the larger system. Each responsible choice we make not only influences our future choices; it also, because of our quantum connectedness, influences the future choices of others as well. Thus, organizations are designed one choice at a time. When we choose acts of kindness, compassion or integrity, they are, in the words of Zohar, "loading the quantum dice" and increasing the probability that others inside and outside the organization will choose to act accordingly.[13] Each of us is in nonlocal correlation with everyone (and everything) else, and each of our decisions influences the entire universe.

The quantum principle of nonseparability puts a new perspective on social responsibility. If everything in the universe is intricately interconnected, what a person does must in some way have a reverse affect on that individual. Therefore, if one wants prosperity in life or in an organization, the first step is to give. In a correlated universe, the more that is given, the more that is received. So-called socially responsible behaviors (e.g., treating all stakeholders respectfully or taking good care of environmental resources) are in actuality merely common sense. We are not only our brothers'/sisters' keepers—we are one with them in an interconnected quantum universe.

Quantum Trusting

The sixth skill, quantum trusting, is derived from chaos theory. Chaos theory provides a new way of viewing change and the turbulence that accompanies it. This theory demonstrates that chaos is inherent in the evolutionary process. It is the catalyst that creates the disequilibrium necessary for system evolution. Chaos is the progenitor of all progress. Without chaos life stagnates and entropy ensues.

Chemistry Nobel prize winner Ilya Prigogine discovered the positive role of chaos by identifying the differences in active and passive chaos.[14] Passive chaos occurs when a closed system reaches equilibrium and its elements move around in a random fashion. Active chaos occurs in an open system that is in a state of disequilibrium. In such a system, environmental feedback serves as a catalyst, disrupting the system and moving that system to higher levels of order and coherency.

The system's new direction appears to be the result of chance and uncertainty. However, a growing number of scientists believe that an invisible ordering principle is at work. British quantum physicist David Bohm's concept of subatomic particles with "quantum potential" suggests that directions received from the quantum field influence the behavior of subatomic particles.[15] Bohm acknowledges that this potential has such complexity that any attempts at prediction are futile; however, our inability to make predictions does not mean that a system's evolution is totally random. It simply means that it cannot be explained.

Bohm's concept of an invisible ordering principle applies to the subatomic world of quantum phenomena. Chaos theory, based on classical physics and applicable to the macroscopic world, has a similar concept, the *strange attractor*. This is a computer term used to trace the evolution of a chaotic system. As chaos theory would predict, a computerized system in chaos behaves in a totally unpredictable manner.

However, over time even the most chaotic systems never go beyond certain phase-space boundaries, the boundary of the strange attractor.

Strange attractors provide visual images of a world in which structure emerges out of chaos. Structured chaos is a remarkable paradox. It suggests that we function in a universe that is both orderly and chaotic, a world that displays structure without clockwork regularity—potentiality without predictability. Authors and educators Margaret Wheatley and Myron Kellner-Rogers reflect on what this might mean for organizations: "If order is for free, we don't have to be the organizers. We don't have to design the world. We don't have to structure existence ... Organization wants to happen."[16]

For many, these ideas are deeply appealing. Many of us are exhausted from our attempts to predict and control. We suspect that there really is a simpler way. Yet we may find ourselves face-to-face with the ego's fear of "letting go and letting God" (as we like to say in Unity). Quantum trusting is the ability to trust life's process—to trust that divine order is always as work. The skill of quantum trusting enables us to ride the rapids of change, fully participating in the adventure without having to control the course; deeply aware that it's easiest to ride a raft in the direction it's headed. As we master this skill, we begin to focus on the mystery of existence, rather than on mastery over it. We become less intent on manipulating life and more intent on simply appreciating it.

Using the skill of quantum trusting is especially challenging in traditional organizations where enormous value is placed on prediction and control. There are, however, many recent organizational processes, like author/consultant Harrison Owen's Open Space Technology,[17] that demonstrate in quantifiable ways the ability of a group of people to quickly self-organize in meaningful and productive ways. Not only are the outcomes of such processes impressive, participants almost always prefer this open design to more traditionally structured options.

Open Space Technology is only one example of what Dee Hock, founder of Visa International, would call "chaordic organization."[18] As leaders individually and collectively begin to use the skill of quantum trusting, many more examples of self-organizing practices will emerge. Championing these practices takes clear intention, strong commitment and a willingness to take the road less traveled. We must be willing to step into the chaotic abyss.

Quantum Being

The final skill, quantum being, recognizes the relational nature of the universe. At the subatomic level, matter comes into being only through relationships. Subatomic particles are abstractions. Their properties are definable and observable only through their interactions with other particles. The probabilities associated with particles are probabilities of relationship. Physics has not, however, always been viewed as a science of relationships. Newton saw particles as distinct entities with rigid boundaries, billiard balls moved around by external forces.[19] Newtonian objects can influence each other's external behavior, but they cannot change each other's internal characteristics. This is not what happens in a quantum relationship, where two particles can actually merge, sharing boundaries and identities and thereby becoming a quantum system that is greater than the sum of the two individual parts.

Quantum relationships are prerequisite to human transformation. It is through relationships that our human potential is released. When we approach relationships with openness and vulnerability, change happens. These quantum encounters often provoke unresolved issues and reopen psychological wounds, thus giving each party the opportunity to learn and heal, or deny and project. As we experience the perceptual transformations that are inherent in quantum relationships, we begin to understand that our outer realities are but a projection of our inner beliefs. Quantum relationships are, therefore, psychological mirrors. In them, individuals can see themselves reflected. When faults are observed in another, those observations are simply mirroring our own issues, providing feedback about unhealed areas of our own psyches.

Quantum being is the ability to be in healthy relationships—relationships based on unconditional love. This skill requires us to own our feelings rather than project them onto others. As we do so, we discover that all relationships are extraordinary learning opportunities. And we begin to suspect that none of them occur without reason. We also discover that those who have the most to teach us are not always our favorite people, but they are valuable contributors to our psychological and spiritual well-being and our organizational effectiveness.

V — New Skills for a New Millennium

If we are to fully integrate the skill of quantum being into our organizations, we must turn our organizational priorities upside down, creating the time and space for dialogue, trusting that improved relationships will translate into improved results. In so doing, we will discover that progress is a by-product of partnership. As we learn these skills, we release our outdated paradigms and we become authentic change masters, changing ourselves and our organizations from the inside out. When enough of us do so, we will create quantum organizations—organizations of purpose and passion. This is my dream for the 21st century. What is yours?

Good Business

Summary

Doing Well and Doing Good
Charlotte Shelton and Martha Lynn

W e trust that this book has helped you to imagine a new way of leading and a new way of being in the workplace. Good business is important not only for the well-being of individuals, it is important for the survival of the planet. Increasingly, old business models based on competition and greed are failing—anyone who has lived through the current recession clearly knows this. Darwin's concept of survival of the fittest makes little sense in a world where our interdependence escalates daily. The world as global village, thanks to technology, is no longer merely a metaphor. It is a fact. And business, as the most powerful and best-resourced institution on the planet, is in many ways setting the rules of the "global village game of life," as Maynard and Mehrtens describe in *The Fourth Wave: Business in the 21st Century:*

> The other institutions of society—political, educational, religious, social—have a decreasing ability to offer effective leadership: their resources limited, their followings fragmented, their legitimacy increasingly questioned. Politicians, academics, priests and proselytizers have neither the resources nor the flexibility to mount an

effective response to the manifold challenges we are facing. Business, by default, must begin to assume responsibility for the whole.[1]

Increasingly, business organizations are stepping up to lead a societal transformation. By modeling corporate social responsibility and leading radical innovation, many businesses are making a difference—in the lives of their customers, their employees and their communities. A few years ago I (Charlotte) visited a remarkable company, Semco, in Sao Paulo, Brazil. In this unionized manufacturing environment, I talked with crusty, middle-age line workers who with tears in their eyes told me about how the remarkable culture of Semco had given them not only a dramatically improved experience of work, it had transformed their home lives too. As the managers of this company transformed their practices from heavy-handed autocracy to a more democratic style, workers' personal lives changed. These line workers began to take some of what they were experiencing at work into their relationships with their wives and children, bringing some democracy into the traditional patriarchal family structure of Brazil. The commitment of Semco's management to organize their business around enlightened practices is sending change waves throughout a society.

I (Martha) have also been fortunate to be part of an organization that dared to do things differently. While working for a large medical center, I was given the opportunity to be part of the team responsible for opening a new hospital in a new market. Under the leadership of a very progressive CEO, we were able to create an organizational structure unlike any other hospital in the city or the region. This structure was not built on traditional "silos," but rather on processes that focused on the customer experience. We selected an advisory board to provide support and oversight; however, the real creation resided with a team of nonmanagement employees. Selection of the team resulted from rigorous interviews focusing on strict criteria. We were specifically looking for seasoned, experienced, exceptional contributors who knew their jobs and had proven success in the trenches. Who better to know processes—what worked and what didn't—than those who lived them every day?

Once chosen, the team's job became that of creating and streamlining processes that focused on the delivery of exceptional customer-focused care. Team members gave up their existing jobs to focus full time on opening the hospital. I could reference numerous stories of the beauty and messiness of the creative process; however, the thing that stood out for me most was the transformation that occurred within each of the team members. The leadership, knowledge, pride, commitment, compassion and dedication brought forth were a bit like the proverbial genie released from a bottle. Team members were asked to contribute in ways never expected, allowed or appreciated in their old jobs. And, once they experienced this creative autonomy, there was no turning back. They knew firsthand what and how they wanted to contribute once the hospital opened, and each accepted a role that would allow his or her true spirit to soar. As with Charlotte's experience at Semco, once people experienced authentic ways of contributing, their lives were influenced in ways too numerous to count.

Call to Action for Business Leaders

Throughout this book you have read many examples of organizations that are doing things differently. You have also read about numerous business practices and personal success strategies that you can apply in your own workplace. The bottom line is this: Nothing happens without a vision. Or, as Scripture suggests, "Without vision, the people perish" (Proverbs 29:18). You now have new images of possibility. What are you going to do with them? What specifically is yours to do to help raise the consciousness of your workplace and, subsequently, your own job satisfaction?

Some of you may be thinking, well, I'm not the CEO, so I can't change what is happening in my workplace. Baloney! We are all leaders, whether we have the title or not. You are unarguably the CEO of your life. Moment by moment, you make choices that create your reality—not only in your personal life, but also at work.

Margaret Wheatley, whose insightful poem can be found in the chapter on "The Leader as Spiritual Agent," reminds us that we don't need leaderless organizations, we need leader-filled ones. We need organizations where everyone is a change agent, changing that which only you can change: your beliefs, your thoughts and your perceptions. And, when enough of us change ourselves, the workplace will change spontaneously. The experiences (and organizations) that we create are merely external projections of our current level of consciousness.

As we begin to take full responsibility for our lives at home and at work, we become what Jean Houston refers to as *people of the breakthrough,* leaders who are willing to align the desires of their heart with their actions. They deeply understand the meaning of the Buddhist saying that "he who knows and does not act, never really knew." John Heider, in his wise book, *The Tao of Leadership,* writes:

If your life works, you influence your family.
If your family works, your family influences the community.
If your community works, your community influences the nation.
If your nation works, your nation influences the world.
If your world works, the ripple effect spreads throughout the cosmos.[2]

We would add a line: If your life works, you create work that is fulfilling and you create workplaces of respect—respect for each other and for the planet.

Creating Socially and Spiritually Responsible Workplaces

For those of us who have seen the recent meltdown of Wall Street and the unemployment on Main Street, we do not need to be told that our current economic system is dysfunctional. For those of us who have seen polluted rivers and toxic dumps, we do not need to be told that our planet's health is in danger. What we do need to remember is this: We can each make a difference! Whether it be redesigning your leadership style, or championing a recycling program in your department, you can help create socially responsible organizations.

You can also help to create spiritually responsible workplaces. Each time you choose to breathe rather than whine, reflect rather than react, or reframe rather than project your negative feelings, you are creating change. By taking full responsibility for the relationships we create at work, we are not only showing spiritual maturity, we are demonstrating our ability to be co-creators of our own experience. As we choose to show up differently at work, we eventually create lives that work and workplaces that thrive.

As Corrine McLaughlin points out in the chapter on "Corporate Social Responsibility," we can indeed do well, individually and collectively, by doing good. As we serve others around us—our customers, our co-workers, our communities—the good deeds we do return to us. We sometimes refer to this as the spiritual law of cause and effect. What we give, we get. Therefore, if we want more prosperity in our individual lives or in our business organizations, we begin by giving generously. Our socially responsible choices are then not only altruistic choices, they are logical choices. These actions come back to us "pressed down and running over."

So whether you are a CEO or a clerk, an accountant or an administrative assistant, will you answer the call? Will you bring more light and love to your workplace? Will you release blame and claim your infinite power as a co-creator with God of a life that works and a workplace that satisfies? This book is your map. How big can you dream? What are you willing to do to make this dream come true? The sky's the limit.

Resources

What Is Unity?

U nity is a worldwide movement of prayer, education and publishing that helps people of all faiths *apply positive spiritual principles in their daily lives.* At its heart, it is a positive, practical, progressive approach to Christianity. Founded in 1889 by Charles and Myrtle Fillmore, Unity teaches the effective daily application of the principles of Truth as taught and exemplified by Jesus Christ. It encourages individuals to take personal responsibility to achieve greater health, love, prosperity, joy and peace in their own lives.

Although Unity considers Jesus Christ to be a great spiritual teacher, the movement honors and respects all spiritual masters and faith traditions. Unity believes that all people are created with sacred worth, and seeks to be of service to anyone seeking spiritual growth and support, regardless of his or her chosen path. Unity has established about 900 centers of study and worship throughout the world, where people discover and practice the Unity principles for creating meaningful and abundant lives.

Unity's Founders

Charles and Myrtle Fillmore discovered New Thought principles in the late 1800s as a result of Myrtle's search for a way to overcome a long-term physical illness—tuberculosis. Her life was transformed in 1886 when she and Charles attended a lecture by Eugene B. Weeks. Mr. Weeks suggested an affirmation and Myrtle began to work with it: "I am a child of God, and therefore I do not inherit sickness." Over time she became free of her disease. Charles, too, began to practice these new principles of prayer and positive thinking. They enabled him to recover from a childhood leg injury. The Fillmores' results were so striking that others began to flock to them for direction. In 1889 Charles and Myrtle founded what is now known as the Unity movement—a worldwide spiritual community committed to positive, practical spiritual teachings.

Today those who visit the 1,400 acres of Unity Village, the home of Unity's world headquarters, can feel the spiritual roots of the legacy Charles and Myrtle Fillmore left us; however, they can also see evidence of their business savvy. From the innovative structural design of the headquarter buildings to the sustainability practices of energy self-sufficiency, there is abundant evidence of their "good business."

Good Business Magazine

Articles From the Great Depression

From the beginning our founders focused Unity on three activities: prayer, publishing and education. One of their early publications was a magazine for the business community, *The Christian Business Man,* launched in July 1922. Though Charles Fillmore was not the editor, he wrote the first article of that first issue titled "Christianity and Commerce." In January 1926 the magazine's name was changed to *Christian Business,* which suggests that Unity's thinking about gender equality was far ahead of business—and of society in general. In July 1933, in the throes of the so-called Great Depression, the name was changed to *Good Business.*

Following are three selected articles from the early issues of *Good Business*: "The Chance of a Lifetime," "Blessings in Disguise" and "Any Job You Want." These articles, written in the depths of the Great Depression, remind us that while we may not always have a "vote" about what happens to our careers, we always have a choice about how we respond. We find these articles as timely for today's economic environment as they were for the 1930s. We hope you do as well!

The Chance of a Lifetime
Mildred R. White

Good Business, February 1934

What would you do if after a long period of unemployment you finally obtained a position that seemed most desirable; and after accepting it, you learned that your new employer engaged in many business practices that were probably within the law, but which were highly unethical according to modern business principles?

You have arrived right where you are for a purpose. You are not shuffled about, hither and thither, carelessly, without a well-formulated plan. Undoubtedly you have been asking for divine guidance to direct you to the right place. And that is where you are. In the beginning do not overlook the fact that since "God is everywhere present," He is in this new position that you have taken and also in your employer who is engaged in unethical practices. This recognition at the start will serve to keep you from condemning or even criticizing the man for whom you work; will preclude your holding the negative thought of ill practice about him.

"But," you insist, "he is not ethical, and if I stay with him I'll have to commit the same infringements of the business code that he carries out in his office." That is a misconception on your part, because no one ever has to do a thing of which his own conscience does not approve.

"Well," you state, "then I'll have to quit, because if I don't carry out his orders he'll let me go anyway."

That part is not for you to worry about—what your employer's reaction to your insistence on right practices might be. Do not even look that far ahead. Certainly you should not let it disturb or alarm you. Go ahead and perform your official duties capably, asking divine direction in exactly what is the honest, Godlike thing to do in every detail of your work. Then let your conscience dictate. If you are led not to carry out certain orders, explain to your employer why you cannot—that they are against your understanding of correct principles. Do not be afraid to refuse. Perhaps he may ask for your resignation. That will be all right. It will merely prove that you have completed the work God had for you to do in that spot, and He will direct you to the next one.

In the meantime, your influence, that of a man who loses a good position rather than sell his birthright for a mess of pottage, will ring for a long time in that other man's life. It may be the one thing needed to change his entire viewpoint, to give him the impetus for a more godly way of living. What is the loss of your salary to that? Especially when you know that God is caring for you and that He will find the right situation in His good time—which means in plenty of time to handle your requirements.

ঌৼৎ

Good Business

It is very likely, however, that the employer not only will not discharge you, but that he may be so convinced of your real worth and honor through this test that he will keep you on your own terms. If this is so, do not be distressed about anything that others do. As long as your own hands are clean, you cannot be tarnished by the practices of others. Refuse to do what you believe wrong. That is the only thing you have to be concerned about. And in this regard let the voice within pass judgment upon what is ethical or unethical.

It is important that you do not lose sight of the fact that no one lives to himself alone. We are constantly bearing witness. Perhaps you are the channel that is to bring Truth to some soul in that office. More people are watching you than you know. Do not avoid any situation where you have been placed after asking for guidance. Simply know that you have a work to perform in that particular spot. Do not shun it by resigning because you do not like their ethics. Better stay where you are and live in such a way that your influence will be felt by all who come in contact with you. Ask yourself this question: "What am I giving this person? Am I spreading God's truth by my conversation, by my actions?"

A married couple came to live near relatives for a short time. The couple was not easy to get along with, and their words did not always ring honest. They made no friends and pestered their relatives until everyone wished them as far away as possible. The couple antagonized and irritated every one until acquaintances avoided being at home when they called and refused to accept invitations to their home.

The day they left town for good, discouraged, dissatisfied, querulous, three women watched them go down the street to the station with a sigh of relief. The fourth looked on and felt a wave of reproach come over her. It had come to her suddenly that she had missed an opportunity. God had brought these people to her for what she could give them, for what she could show them of the perfection of His life.

She looked back over the three months the couple had been in town and realized that not once in all that time had she given them love. Not once had she demonstrated to them by an understanding sympathy the Christ way of living. Instead they had appeared unlovable, even undesirable, and she had denied them the help she now knew she had been supposed to give, the help that would have brought their real divinity into evidence, if she had looked beyond their apparently disagreeable traits to their God selves. And as she knew, sadly, that they probably would not pass her way again, that she had lost her one chance to help these particular children of God, she resolved never again to miss her opportunity.

And so this may be the contact that will cause your employer to about-face. Recognize it as such. Do not worry about the results. Simply remain where you are and live the God life. It is quite probable that your steadfastness will change the actual business ethics of the entire organization. At least know that you have something to do where you are, for God. And with this consciousness and with eagerness to follow His bidding, you will not be removed until you have accomplished your aim, and then only to go up higher.

Blessings in Disguise

Mara Lowman

Good Business, July 1933

What at the time we regarded as a disaster so often proves to have been a blessing in disguise that it will generally pay us to learn to look on every event as for our good. Untold energy will be saved when we are able to accept apparent losses philosophically. Furthermore, we shall find our eyes wider open to new opportunities, opportunities that lead to heights greater than we could have achieved in any other way.

Just look back over your own life. Do you not remember more than one success that you can trace as directly rising out of an apparent failure of one kind or another? Maybe it was a job you lost. You felt the whole world had crashed about your ears! But after a while you found another job, a brand-new opportunity, providing you with vastly greater prospects for advancement. Through a piece of seeming hard luck you thus found yourself transferred to an environment where you were able to forge steadily ahead, actually getting somewhere on the road to success.

∾

It takes a stiff jolt sometimes to get us out of a rut. I know whereof I speak, for I went through the experience myself. It was long before I had made the marvelous discovery of Truth. Through certain circumstances, which I now know to have been built up through my own mental pattern, I lost a valued position that I had held and advanced in for six years. With the loss of the position, I lost all faith in myself. I was utterly beaten. It took me nearly two years, during which I merely dilly-dallied indefinitely, to awake at last to the realization that I, and I only, was responsible for my seeming failure.

Instead of defeat, here was opportunity knocking at my door. I had advanced as far as I cared to go in that old job. I had been dissatisfied with it, yet had held on to it as the easiest way. Forced out of the rut at last, I was still clinging. The new light struck me with the dazzling force of sunlight entering a long-darkened room. I squared my shoulders, flung up my chin, and with a prayer on my lips set out on the trail of the new position that I suddenly knew was awaiting me. Of course I found it! The result of my new mental outlook was as natural as day following night.

For the next two years I enjoyed a position equal in advantages and advancement to my fondest dreams. Then, owing to financial conditions, there came a cutting down of the staff that eventually reached me. But my lesson was learned. I searched beneath the surface, to bring to light a growing interest in and an inclination toward another line of work, which was similar to that of my profession, yet dissimilar enough so that I had not been able to find time in which to combine the two. This time, you see, I was able to analyze.

Instead of a sense of loss and terror at being thrown once again on a market glutted with my type of services, I experienced a feeling of joy and opportunity, a great certainty that good was mine. I am now preparing myself for it.

I wish that everyone in the seemingly desperate situation of unemployment could catch the vision that has come to me. Look on an event as loss or failure, and such it becomes. No openings? Not enough jobs to go round? Those in a position to know assure us that there are enough jobs in the world for everyone. Every job that machinery or modern methods have displaced has, if we will but look for it, its counterpart in some new kind of occupation. The human mind and body are rich. There is no limit to the new abilities that we may develop, to say nothing of perfecting the old ones.

Let old doors close. The experiences behind them have served their purpose, built a foundation for what is ahead.

But let us go back. Perhaps it is some other kind of loss that you are feeling most keenly right now, the loss of material possessions such as, for instance, your home? Or should I not say rather "your house;" for home is spirit. More than a year ago my sister appeared to have lost her home. She was just beginning the study of Truth and was working to build up a prosperity consciousness involving steadier employment for her husband and thus making possible the good surroundings that they wanted their children to enjoy.

When the bailiff walked in and seized all their belongs to satisfy back rent that my brother-in-law had not been able to pay, it seemed momentarily as though the whole world had crashed about their ears. No home, no possessions, no money.

Could a situation appear more desperate than this? Yet help rushed in from every side. Opportunities unforeseen, undreamed of, appeared. Work came where no work had been before. Opportunity came to rent an ideal home, with advantages not before enjoyed, at an unusually reasonable cost. Piece by piece came furnishings as gifts, or they were purchased at minimum prices.

Who could foresee the blessings that would rise out of this apparent loss? Had they given in, given up, how blinded they would have been by negative emotions, their own sense of failure and defeat. But they kept their spirit of home and prosperity intact. One door they shut behind them in the faith that other doors would open down the corridor of life.

Are there not other doors awaiting us all? Loss of employment, loss of home or other material possessions, loss of health, even, may mean only that the laws of adjustment are forcing you into new pathways of development. Before you label happenings negatively, look for the new door. You may have received a blessing in disguise!

Any Job You Want

Gardner Hunting

Good Business, February 1934

You can have any job you want. You do not believe that, do you? That is why you do not get the job you want now; you do not believe you can get it. Did you ever hear Mark Twain's advice to the young seeker after a job? He said something like this: "Pick out the man you want to work for, and then go and work for him. Tell him you are going to work for him for nothing till he decides you are worth something, and how much." That seems an absurd piece of advice. But it will certainly work if you really put it into practice. Now, think a moment with me.

If you get a job—any sort of a job—what will your employer pay you for? For the work you do, of course. Will he pay you in advance? He will not. He will pay you after you have worked a month, a week, a day. How much will he pay you? What you earn, of course. Will he pay you more than you are worth—even if he has agreed to? He will not. If you do not measure up to specifications, he will get out of his agreement in one way or another. He will discharge you, or if he has made a contract with you, he will break it or make you break it, or make your situation intolerable, or buy you off. He will certainly not pay you for something you do not give him.

Here is that saying in the business world again, that you cannot get something for nothing. You cannot. This means that you cannot get salary or wages for something you do not do. Do you think you see men getting paid for something they are not delivering? Watch them. Watch the loafers and the quitters and the "soldiers."

But there is a deeper thing under this fact and these appearances than people commonly think. It is this: Justice! Justice does work in the affairs of men, whether they recognize it or not. You do not believe it? Study it. Men do get what they want—what they really want. You can get what you really want, as we have said—and you will get it, whether you know it or not!

"But," you say, "just as many good men have failed of their aim as have succeeded." So? What does it mean to be "good"? Goodness, in the ordinary sense, has nothing to do with the matter. If it had, we could not understand the situation at all. People who try to explain success or failure on the ground of goodness never do understand it—nor anything else they try to explain on the same ground. Because "goodness" or "badness" in the ordinary moral sense is not the reason. Law is the reason, for everything.

"Whatsoever ye shall ask in prayer, believing, ye shall receive." Real virtue consists in keeping in harmony with the law—or trying to. Goodness, in this sense, is always rewarded, and badness, in the same sense, is always punished. That is, the law works for those who keep it and works against those who choose to go against it. I do not dare to set any limits. I do not believe there are any limits. It does not make the least difference in the world whether we know the law or not: it works. "Ignorance of the law is no excuse." And you cannot blame some far-off God for your actions, or for anything that happens to you, or for your knowing the law or not knowing it. It is up to you!

Does that frighten you? Or, if you believed it, would it frighten you? Instead of frightening you, it should encourage you, inspirit you, stir you up to your highest ambition, fill you with your highest hope, assure you of realization of your highest desire, make you certain of success, and happy beyond your dreams! Because you cannot lose!

Now, let us see. We have made some pretty rash statements, have we not? From the ordinary, unbelieving standpoint, yes. But it is not bumptiousness to state law, nor modesty to understate it. What have we said? You can have anything you really want. Well, you can; the thing you want is among the possibilities for you or you would not want it. Desire is implanted in you by a power that intends you to have what that desire calls for. You have no desires that this power has not given you. Desire was meant to be fulfilled—consuming, supreme desire, not the piddling little wishes that do not even last overnight or past mealtime. Your real desire becomes the great purpose of your life; and it matters not what that purpose is, you are going to get a reward commensurate with your single-heartedness. Besides, your desire is implanted in you by this power we are talking about.

This power will grant the desire—has already granted it—because this power is the only power there is in the universe. It is the power for which another name is God. He is the only power you will ever know, and the only power you will ever get a job from; the only power you will ever work for and the only power that will ever pay you. You may think you ask some man or woman for a job, but you do not really. You "ask" the universal law for that job. And because the universal law (God) has put the desire for that job in you, you will get it. And because that same universal law is the paymaster you will get paid for it, and no man or woman on earth can prevent it. You are working for God not man. God is the one to whom you go for your job, for whom you labor, from whom you receive your reward. You cannot help it; that is the way it is. It is so, whether you believe it or not, whether you know it or not, whether you like it or not!

But you remind me that I have said that all desire comes from God. It may be well enough to think that the desire to work comes from the one power, but does the desire of the sitter to sit come also from the Supreme Being? Why, certainly! In Him I live, and move, and have being; I have nothing without Him. Yes, even my desire to sit! But who is God? Why, God is my being. God is my life, my strength, my intelligence, my mind. Now turn the statement around. My being is God, my life is God, my intelligence is God, my mind is

God. Do you pretend to say that you have a desire independent of your mind? Hardly. Well, that is the answer.

The answer is that God, instead of being something outside of you, is within you, controlling all your affairs through you. I begin to believe that you have only to realize that overwhelming conception in order to have God come forth visibly into your affairs, whatever they are, whoever you are, wherever you are, whatever your circumstances appear to be. You are an individual expression of God. You create what you choose. How? First by thinking it. That is the only way anything is created—by thought. If you think that things are created by hammer and nails, or steam shovels, or dynamos, or lathes, or trowels, or giant powder, or printing presses, or congresses, or kings, you have never thought even so far back as the drafting table or blue pencil!

Things are created by thought in the mind, and by nothing else and nowhere else. Yes, by your thought, and in your mind. And when you begin to realize that, you will begin to work for the God who is universal Mind, in you and in me and everybody else, and in everything in the universe. You will realize that you cannot fail to do what you really want to do and have what you really want to have.

How shall you begin? By going after that first job with an idea in your mind just the reverse of what you have been trying to hold there. Think not about what you are going to get, but about what you can give. Ask for opportunity to give, and give with all your heart all you have got, knowing that you cannot fail to get back what you give out. For who are you? You are the expression of God in your individuality.

Think of that. In Him you live and move and have your being. You are one with God, the supreme power in the universe. You are one with supreme universal Mind. And universal Mind creates what it wants to create. In other words, it gives out what it wants to see manifested. Think of it. Think! You! Not somebody else—you! You cannot fail!

Daily Affirmations for Good Business

Good Business magazine, in addition to professional development articles and business success stories, contained a daily good business principle. Readers were encouraged to put the daily principle into practice by pausing at noon each day to read the affirmation and meditate on it for a few minutes. Below is a month's worth of daily good business principles for you to practice. These daily affirmations are adopted from the early issues of *Good Business* magazine. We encourage you to use them month after month until they become a habitual part of the way you do business.

Day 1: I fairly sizzle with zeal and enthusiasm as I do all that which is mine to do.

Day 2: I face every challenge with confidence.

Day 3: I see only the best in my co-workers.

Day 4: I learn from all my experiences.

Day 5: I appreciate new opportunities to learn and grow.

Day 6: I thrive on change.

Day 7: I take full responsibility for all my thoughts, feelings and actions.

Day 8: I always show up with integrity.

Day 9: I provide first-class service to everyone with whom I interact.

Resources

Day 10: I show compassion to others.

Day 11: I welcome constructive feedback. It helps me grow.

Day 12: I take time daily to listen for inner guidance.

Day 13: I bring a sense of mindfulness to all decisions.

Day 14: I am a self-observer. I am conscious of how my thoughts, feelings and behaviors affect others.

Day 15: I ask questions and listen before I speak in emotionally charged situations.

Day 16: I am committed to win-win conflict resolution.

Day 17: I demonstrate my faith in the goodness of life, even in challenging times.

Day 18: I trust in divine order—even when I wish things were different.

Day 19: I courageously choose love—in every situation.

Day 20: With each decision I make, I consider its impact on others.

Day 21: I think "green," and I act accordingly.

Day 22: I expect abundance in my life.

Day 23: I expect abundance for my organization.

Day 24: I am a wise steward of the resources entrusted to me.

Day 25: I am poised and peaceful. Nothing can disturb my peace of mind.

Day 26: I move through the challenges of today with ease and grace.

Day 27: I give liberally and joyously of my time and talents.

Day 28: I am open and authentic in all my interactions.

Day 29: I can always be trusted to tell the truth.

Day 30: I am open to new ideas.

Additional Affirmations

I will learn something new today.

I am grateful for the good I have received.

I express enthusiasm for my work.

I cultivate teamwork.

I serve myself by serving others.

I radiate cheerfulness.

I sow seeds of kindness.

I make helpfulness a daily practice.

I encourage others to express their greatness.

I choose to be a channel for divine intelligence.

I see only possibilities.

I demonstrate a willingness to give and receive.

I embrace diversity.

I see myself as unlimited.

I am focused yet flexible.

I count the blessings of my job.

I find a new opportunity to serve.

I release past regrets and anxieties about the future. I live in the now.

I live my values and use them to make all decisions.

I find meaning and purpose in my work.

I take time to play and pray.

I am fully alive. I feel invigorated.

I release mediocrity. I do my best in tasks both large and small.

I set a good example in all that I do.

I use discernment as well as data as I make decisions.

I am merciful and kind.

Resources

I extol the virtues of others.

I am a radiating center of peace and goodwill.

I rejoice in the opportunity to give.

I bring new zest to my work.

I make a list of my blessings and think about them throughout the day.

I exemplify the spirit of cooperation.

I take time to activate my connection with the divine.

I act on principle by aligning my thoughts, beliefs and actions.

I give credit where credit is due.

I find joy in all I do.

I live abundantly. I have no resource limitations.

I am guided by infinite wisdom.

Divine love prospers me.

I am successful in all that I undertake.

Good Business Clubs

In the 1920s and 30s *Good Business* clubs sprang up in over 100 cities, from Boston to Los Angeles, as well as in Canada, Great Britain and Scotland. These clubs were a part of the Christian Business Federation, though the principles espoused are congruent with all spiritual paths.

We encourage you to consider forming a Good Business club—whether Christian or interfaith—in your own organization, neighborhood or place of worship. Below you will find 40 discussion questions that could be used at these gatherings. The essays in this book, written by contemporary business writers, thinkers and practitioners, as well as the personal experiences members of your group have as they use the daily business affirmations, also make good discussion material.

1. How do the decisions in your organization affect the larger world?

2. How can we learn to integrate our spiritual paths and our career paths?

3. How has the spiritual principle of giving and receiving worked for you personally and professionally?

4. How can we shift our outdated paradigms (ideas/beliefs)?

5. How do we learn to view all challenges as opportunities?

6. What would you need to change in order to show up each day at work with joy and vitality?

7. What do you most appreciate about your work?

8. How do you approach tedious tasks with ease and grace?

9. How do you work cooperatively with highly opinionated co-workers?

10. Is there anything about your work that triggers fear? If so, how might you replace fear with faith?

11. How do you differentiate between divine ideas and ego-driven ideas?

12. What are the key factors that have contributed to your success thus far? What actions might you take to be even more successful?

13. Are you living up to your career potential? If not, why not?

14. How does blessing a person, circumstance or event impact our relationship to them or it?

15. What from your past is currently affecting your career, either positively or negatively?

16. What role does vision play in the attainment of success?

17. How do we cultivate spiritual vision?

18. Do your actions always align with your core values? If not, how can you close the gap?

19. What one big decision would you make if you just knew how to implement it?

20. Which is easier for you: focus or flexibility? How can you strengthen the weaker quality without diminishing the stronger one?

21. Where do you want your career to be in one year? Five years? Ten years? What immediate action are you willing to take to move in the direction of your goals?

22. Which is easier for you: competition or cooperation? Is this working for you?

23. Is there a relationship between science and spirituality? What relevance do these disciplines have in the workplace?

24. Is it possible for individuals and organizations to do well financially while also doing good in the world? Examples?

25. What role do persistence and perseverance play in career success?

26. What effect does faith have on success?

27. What is the nature of personal power?

28. How do we manifest only good in our lives and our careers?

29. How does serving others serve us?

Resources
~

30. How do you communicate with Divine Intelligence/
    Infinite Mind/God? Does such communication have a
    place at work?

31. How do you release negative ideas and false beliefs?

32. What is required of those who seek spiritual mastery
    as well as career success?

33. Why is anger rarely useful?

34. Does love have a place in the workplace?

35. Do you believe that your workplace is populated with
    villains and victims? How so?

36. How do you stay peaceful amidst the storms of orga-
    nizational chaos?

37. How can spiritual principles help us manage time
    more effectively?

38. Is your organization a good citizen of its community
    and the planet? If yes, describe how. If no, what could
    be done differently?

39. Are partnership and teamwork easy for you?

40. Are you bringing your best self to work or are you
    merely going through the motions?

~

Endnotes

Introduction

[1]Martinek, Frank. *Good Business.* July 1933: 20.

[2]Fillmore, Charles. *The Christian Business Man.* July 1922: 7.

Chapter 2

This article is adapted from Corinne McLaughlin's *The Practical Visionary*, Unity Village, MO: Unity House Books, 2010.

[1]Broadway, Bill. "Good for the Soul—and for the Bottom Line: More Companies Are Promoting Spirituality in the Workplace and Finding It Pays." *Washington Post.* August 19, 2001: A01.

[2]Verschoor, Curtis. "Principles Build Profits." *Management Accounting.* October 1997: 42.

[3]"Religion in the Workplace." *Business Week.* November 1, 1999. <http://www.businessweek.com/careers/content/jan1990/b36 53001.htm>

[4]*Corporate Social Responsibility Newswire.* United Nations Global Compact press release. July 5, 2007.

[5]"Religion in the Workplace," *Business Week.*

[6]*ABC Evening News.* February 25, 1998.

[7]Newsome, Melba. "Hey Reverend, Let's Do Lunch." *U.S. News and World Report.* January 23, 2005. <http://www.usnews.com/ usnews/biztech/articles/050131/31eechaplain.htm>

[8]"Ministers Tend the Flock at Worksites." *Los Angeles Times.* July 30, 2007 http://www.articles.latimes.com/2007/jul/30/ business/ft-chaplains30

[9]"Religion in the Workplace," *Business Week.*

[10]"Energy: Blowing in the Wind." *Newsweek.* March 13, 2006. <http://www.newsweek.com/id/46907>

[11]Gibran, Kahlil. *The Prophet.* Alfred A. Knopf, 1997: 27-28.

Chapter 3

[1]Sisodia, Rajendra S., David B. Wolfe, and Jagdish N. Sheth. *Firms of Endearment: How World-Class Companies Profit From Passion and Purpose.* Upper Saddle River, NJ: Wharton School Publishing, 2007.

[2]*Firms of Endearment: How World-Class Companies Profit From Passion and Purpose,* Sisodia and Wolfe.

[3]Mitroff, Ian, and Elizabeth A. Denton. *A Spiritual Audit of Corporate America: A Hard Look at Spirituality, Religion and Values in the Workplace.* San Francisco: Jossey-Bass, 1999.

Chapter 4

This article is adapted from Riane Eisler, *The Real Wealth of Nations: Creating a Caring Economics,* San Francisco: Berrett-Koehler, 2007, 2008.

[1]Burud, Sandra, and Marie Tomolo. *Leveraging the New Human Capital: Adaptive Strategies, Results Achieved and Stories of Transformation.* Mountain View, CA: Davies-Black Publishing, 2004: 23.

[2]"FSB/WINNING WORKPLACES, Best Bosses 2004: Distinguished Finalists." Retrieved from <http://www.winningworkplaces.org/bestbossesaward/previouswin_2004_fnl.php>

[3]*The Retention Dilemma.* Hay Group, 2001. <www.haygroup.com/library/index.asp>.

[4]Santa Barbara United Way survey, 2000. <http://www.unitedwaysb.org/worklife.html>.

[5]Circadian survey, 2003. <http://www.circadian.com/media/Release-03Aug12.html>.

[6]*Life's Work: Generational Attitudes Toward Work and Life Integration.* Radcliffe Institute for Advanced Study, 2000. <www.Radcliffe.edu/research/pubpol/lifeswork.pdf>.

[7]*The Most Important Work-Life Related Studies.* Work and Family Connection, 2005. <http://www. familiesandwork.org/>.

[8]*Leveraging the New Human Capital: Adaptive Strategies, Results Achieved and Stories of Transformation,* Burud and Tomolo.

[9]*Life's Work: Generational Attitudes Toward Work and Life Integration.* Radcliffe Institute for Advanced Study, 2000.

Endnotes

❧

[10]Ibid.

[11]Ibid.

[12]Bright Horizons Child Care Trends, 2002. <http://www.child-careinhealthcare.org/employer-sponsored-child-care.php>.

[13]*Leveraging the New Human Capital: Adaptive Strategies, Results Achieved and Stories of Transformation*, Burud and Tomolo.

Chapter 9

This essay is adapted from Peter Block's book *Community: The Structure of Belonging* (Berrett-Koehler: San Francisco, May 2008).

Chapter 10

Excerpted from Richard Barrett's upcoming book: *The New Leadership Agenda: A full-spectrum, values-based approach to leadership development and leadership coaching* (working title).

[1]Harman, Willis. *Global Mind Change*. Grand Central Publishing, 1990.

[2]Turchin, Peter. *Historical Dynamics: Why States Rise and Fall*. Princeton, NJ: Princeton University Press, 2003.

[3]Barrett, Richard. *Building a Values-driven Organizations: A Whole System Approach to Cultural Transformation*. Boston: Butterworth-Heinemann, 2006.

[4]Beinhocker, E. *Strategy at the Edge of Chaos*. McKinsey Quarterly, 1997. Vol. 1:25-39.

[5]*Strategy at the Edge of Chaos*, Beinhocker.

[6]Kotter, John P., and James L. Heskett. *Corporate Culture and Performance*. New York: The Free Press, 1992.

Chapter 11

[1]Palmer, Parker. *The Active Life—A Spirituality of Work, Creativity and Caring*. San Francisco: Harper & Row, 1990: 44.

[2]Ibid.

Chapter 12

[1]Anthony, Bobbi. American Society for Quality study cited in *Practicing Out of the Box*. Dental Economics, 2004. Vol 94; Part 5: 50-55.

❧

[2]Coffman, Curt, and Gabriel Gonzales-Molina. *Follow This Path: How the World's Greatest Organizations Drive Growth by Unleashing Human Potential.* Warner Books, 2002.

[3]Branham, Leigh, and Mark Hirschfeld. *Re-Engage: How America's Best Places to Work Inspire Extra Effort in Extraordinary Times.* McGraw-Hill, 2010.

Chapter 13

[1]Kinjerski, V., and B.J. Skrypnek. *The Promise of Spirit at Work: Increasing Job Satisfaction and Organizational Commitment and Reducing Turnover and Absenteeism in Long-term Care.* Journal of Gerontological Nursing, 2008. 43(10): 17-27.

Chapter 14

[1]Nemeth, Maria. *Mastering Life's Energies.* Novato, CA: New World Library, 2007.

[2]Sharp Paine, Lynn. *Value Shift: Why Companies Must Merge Social and Financial Imperatives to Achieve Superior Performance.* McGraw-Hill, 2003: 7.

[3]Barrett, Richard. *Liberating the Corporate Soul—Building a Visionary Organization.* Butterworth-Heinemann, 1998: 109.

[4]Ibid.

[5]Ibid.

[6]Ibid.

[7]Barrett, Richard. *Building a Values-Driven Organization: A Whole System Approach to Cultural Transformation.* Butterworth-Heinemann, 2006: 110.

Chapter 15

Part of this chapter first appeared in *Boston Women's Business* (March 2004) as part of the article "Revitalize Post-Downsize with New Emphasis" by Debora Jackson. Used with permission of the publisher.

Chapter 21

[1]Canfield, Jack, and Jacqueline Miller. *Heart at Work.* McGraw Hill, 1996: 8.

Endnotes

[2]Williamson, Marianne. *A Return to Love: Reflections on the Principles of A Course in Miracles.* HarperCollins, 1992. Chapter 7, Section 3: 190-191.

3Gibran, Kahlil. *The Prophet.* Alfred A. Knopf, 1997: 27-28.

Chapter 22

This article is adapted from Charlotte Shelton's book *Quantum Leaps: 7 Skills for Workplace ReCreation.* Butterworth-Heinemann, 1999.

[1]Zukav, Gary. *The Dancing Wu Li Masters: An Overview of the New Physics.* New York: Bantam Books, 1979.

[2]Csikszentmihalyi, Mihaly. *Flow: The Psychology of Optimal Experience.* New York: HarperCollins, 1990.

[3]McNeill, Daniel, and Paul Freiberger. *Fuzzy Logic.* New York: Simon and Schuster, 1994.

[4]*IHM Research Update.* Boulder Creek, CA: Institute of HeartMath, Vol. 1, No. 1., 1993.

[5]Childre, Doc Lew. *Cut-Thru: Achieve Total Security and Maximum Energy.* Boulder Creek, CA: Planetary Publications, 1996.

[6]Capra, Fritjof. *The Tao of Physics* (2nd ed.). Boulder: Shambhala, 1983

[7]Zohar, Danah. *The Quantum Self: Human Nature and Consciousness Defined by the New Physics.* New York: William Morrow, 1990.

[8]Wald, George. "Life and Mind in the Universe." *International Journal of Quantum Chemistry; Quantum Biology Symposium,* 1984: 1-2.

[9]Houston, Jean. *The Possible Human: A Course in Extending Your Physical, Mental, and Creative Abilities.* Los Angeles: J.P. Tarcher, 1982.

[10]McCarthy, Kathleen. "Uncertainty Is a Blessing, Not a Bane," *APA Monitor,* September, 1994: 28.

[11]Lloyd, Seth. "Quantum-Mechanical Computers." *Scientific American,* October, 1995: 144.

[12]Gribbin, John. *In Search of Schroedinger's Cat: Quantum Physics and Reality.* New York: Bantam Books, 1984.

[13]*The Quantum Self: Human Nature and Consciousness Defined by the New Physics,* Zohar.

[14]Prigogine, Ilya, and Isabelle Stengers. *Order Out of Chaos: Man's New Dialogue With Nature*. Boulder: Shambhala, 1984.

[15]Briggs, John, and Peat, F. David. *Turbulent Mirror: An Illustrated Guide to Chaos Theory and the Science of Wholeness*. New York: Harper and Row, 1989.

[16]Wheatley, Margaret, and Myron Kellner-Rogers. *A Simpler Way*. San Francisco: Berrett-Koehler, 1996.

[17]Owen, Harrison. *Expanding Our Now: The Story of Open Space Technology*. San Francisco: Berrett-Koehler, 1997.

[18]Waldrop, M. Mitchell. "The Trillion-Dollar Vision of Dee Hock," *Fast Company*, Issue 5, 1996: 75.

[19]*The Quantum Self: Human Nature and Consciousness Defined by the New Physics*, Zohar.

Summary

[1]Maynard, Herman Bryant Jr., and Susan E. Mehrtens. *The Fourth Wave: Business in the 21st Century*. San Francisco: Berrett-Koehler, 1993: 97.

[2]Heider, John. *The Tao of Leadership: Lao Tzu's Te Ching Adapted for a New Age*. Atlanta: Humanics New Age, 1985: 107.

About the Editors

Charlotte Shelton, Ed.D., is president/CEO of Unity, an international transdenominational organization dedicated to helping people apply positive spiritual principles in their daily lives. She was previously Chair of the Management and Marketing Division at Rockhurst University, Kansas City, Missouri, and president of WiseWork Coaching and Consulting. She is the author of *Quantum Leaps: 7 Skills for Workplace ReCreation* and co-author of *The NeXt Revolution: What Gen X Women Want at Work and How Their Boomer Bosses Can Help Them Get It.*

Martha Lynn, Ph.D., has held executive positions in a variety of industries, including financial institutions, a national engineering and architectural firm, and a regional health care system. Martha was a partner in HCAP International, a consulting business, before joining Unity. As the vice president of SpiritPath at Unity Village, her responsibilities include oversight of Unity's hotel and conference center, retreats, events and workshops, weddings and meeting planning, the Unity Bookstore and Coffee Shop and Unity Inn.

B0091